PHILIP H. ASHBY is the author of *The Conflict of Religions*. He received his B.D. from the Pacific School of Religion and his Ph.D. from the University of Chicago. In 1958, Dr. Ashby took part in the State Department Foreign Leader's Exchange Program in India. He was Jonathan Edwards Preceptor of Princeton University for study in India and Ceylon in 1953. At present, he is Associate Professor of Religion at Princeton University.

HISTORY AND FUTURE
OF RELIGIOUS
THOUGHT

HISTORY AND FUTURE OF RELIGIOUS THOUGHT

CHRISTIANITY

HINDUISM

BUDDHISM

ISLAM

PHILIP H. ASHBY

Prentice-Hall, Inc. *Englewood Cliffs, N.J.*

A SPECTRUM BOOK

Library of Congress Catalog Card No. 63-15411

Printed in the United States of America

C

To Kelley

CONTENTS

HISTORY AND FUTURE OF RELIGIOUS THOUGHT

I
The
Mandate
of the
Present

In the history of the world, religion in widely different forms has been a basic element in society and individual life. It is the nature of most men to look beyond themselves and their society. Much of the sanction for their collective activities has derived from the beliefs which the religious sensitivities of men have produced. Today the vision may be blurred to the extent that individuals and their societies are in confusion. But religion remains, either potent or impotent, as a factor not yet totally dismissed by society or by men. Both look to it even as they sometimes deny it, and in the denial the perceptive observer often notes an element of despair that what they disavow is gone and has not been replaced.

Given this fundamental importance of religion to individual life and corporate society, it is obvious that serious consideration must be directed toward an understanding of religion in its universal and particular manifestations and their implications. The study of the history of the world's religions continues to supply us with growing insight into, and appreciation of, the varied religious experience of humanity. It is being demonstrated today that contemporary religions cannot be understood adequately in relation to the present and the future if consideration is limited to their past geographic and cultural areas. While some of these religions have at times been thought to be limited to a people, their followers have not believed that their presuppositions and teachings were limited in their universal truth.

Our increasing knowledge of the history and culture of areas other than our own continues to demonstrate that while each society has in the past been to some extent a unit in itself, its unity

1

did not preclude a relationship and often a dependence upon that which on the surface appears to be foreign. Culture is by nature an absorbent, and as such it is composed often of elements which have their origin beyond the established unity of the culture. It is hardly necessary to say that the same is true in the case of religion. Its origins, its development, its presuppositions, its expression in words, action, art, and social structure—all reflect to varying degree the influence and guidance of elements which in origin and development are not identified exclusively with the religion's own theologically understood beginnings and conception of its unity.

In its recurring themes, highly developed religion is not to be limited to or circumscribed by the local or particular nature of its initial and subsequent provincial religious experience. Once a religion possesses a tenure of unity with a society which is not isolated, it is brought into an atmosphere of fluidity and novelty wherein its capability to respond is challenged. Those religions which do not possess the ability to respond to that which is different from the unity which has historically supported them do not survive. Those which do, continue to be of significance to their adherents and to the society with which they are associated. Religions which are able not only to exist in such circumstances but to continue and often increase their contributions to their adherents, are subjected to a process which causes them to look back to their beginnings at the same time they are being enriched by the new events which confront them.

1

It is because such religions are involved in the struggle to be meaningful and contemporaneous that their theologies have been and continue to be produced. There have been initial embryo theologies that were implied in the myths, legends, and revelations which are integral to a religion. Each religion of significance today has had its period or periods of intellectual excitement wherein what has been assumed has been made explicit, and what has been doubted has either been established or rejected. But it has been particularly under the spur of attack and novelty that each of the world's great religions has produced its predominant and most significant theological thought. Though in each case the situation was different; the Nagarjunas of Buddhism, the Augustines of Christianity, the Shankaras of Hinduism, the Ghazzalis of Islam, and the Maimonides of Judaism—whether heterodox or orthodox—were responding to a conscious need of their religion in their time. The Suzukis, Barths, Radhakrishnans, Muhammad Iqbals, and Bubers of this century follow in the footsteps of their theological predecessors, similarly conscious of the need to articulate their religious faith in terms which are meaningful to the present culture and defensible before the attacks of its enemies.

It is theology, therefore, which today must face the facts of the present world condition and the relation of the religion which it represents to that condition. It is theology and its handmaidens, the Philosophy of Religion and the History of Religion, which must apply themselves to the important task of expressing in meaningful terms the universal and particular relevance of religion to the needs and aspirations of contemporary man. No longer can theology be content to seek to demonstrate the applicability of religious faith within its traditional boundaries alone. And while it may rightly be maintained that theology has not consciously thought of itself as speaking within a limited arena of concern, identified only with the geographic boundaries of the faith, yet we are forced to admit that the history of the world's theologies is primarily a chronicle of preoccupation with concerns within the particular religion and its related culture. However, it was often spurs from outside the unity of the religion and its society that caused the great theologies to be created. The degree to which they were concerned only with defense created their limitations; the measure in which they recognized themselves to be involved with universal matters everywhere applicable to particular situations, brought into being their potential world-wide significance.

The present-day religious thinker will of necessity be compelled to deal with matters which are pre-eminently within his religious faith and its traditions. He cannot, and should not, avoid those problems which are essential to a further understanding and clarification of the religion with which he is identified. A religion is never free of its responsibility to make clear to its adherents in every generation the significance of its teaching. It must state its basic presuppositions concerning the nature of the Divine, the character of Man, and the structure of Existence. Not only must these doctrines and the articles of belief which derive from them be taught to men and women within the faith, but they must also be made intelligible and defensible in the light of the total knowledge which is integral to the society and culture with which the adherents are also identified. Theology is therefore in conversation with philosophy, with ethics, with science and its resulting technology, with the arts—with the myriad elements which combine to support and structure a society and its culture. The role of the theologian and religious philosopher in any contemporary religion is by its nature unlimited in its range, even within the strictures apparently associated with the traditional religion in which he works.

True, theologians of the past have not conceived themselves to be working under limitations, either as to the universal scope of the problems with which they were wrestling or the eternal and cosmic significance of the truth they were seeking to understand more fully. It must be recognized that the concerns of religion are directed to the whole of existence, as any particular religion conceives of existence. Even at those points where a religion appears to be silent in its teachings, or its injunctions, its silence does not so much indicate a conscious lack of jurisdiction or concern as much as it reveals a deliberate decision as to the relative unimportance of the matter.

The religious thinker of the twentieth century is not different from his predecessors. The degree to which he has ignored the present world situation is a reflection of his inherited provincialism more than it is an indication of his lack of solicitude. Be he a Buddhist bikkshu, a Hindu philosopher or sanyasi, a Muslim, Jewish, or Christian theologian, he maintains that the religious thought he is seeking to explicate is universal in its significance and its application to human life. His error is not so much in his conception of his task; it more often is in his failure to lift his thought above the traditional usages to which it has been limited in the past.

There would appear to be little need today to argue for the necessity of breaking the bonds of the theological and general religious provincialisms remaining from the past. Any justification for them which may possibly have been defensible no longer exists.

The geographic separations of yesterday have in most, if not all, cases been relative only. Few, if any, religions existed only to themselves for any appreciable period of time. Even in their periods of unchallenged authority within a given area, they were not immune from the overt and covert influences of other religious thought within and beyond their borders. Today the same is true to an even greater extent. The technological, economic, and political interrelatedness of the world has brought all religions into confrontation with one another. What in the past has existed only at various times within large regional bounderies is now a world condition.

What does this mean for the theologian, for the philosopher of religion, and for the historian of religion? We have suggested that he cannot and should not disassociate himself from the concerns and problems of his own religious faith. We would further submit that the issues of his faith can be confronted adequately only when he seeks, by every legitimate means, to break out beyond the inherited religious restrictions which have prevented him from encountering seriously the problems which the universality and particularity of his religious claims bring to light.

It is obvious that the theologian and philosopher of religion inherit a specific religious past. This inheritance is positive to the degree and manner in which it leads to affirmative religious belief and understanding. It serves to guide and establish religious perspective. The inheritance is also negative. A positive element of thought automatically produces its negative counterpart, and the negation will often be as decisive in the formulation of the belief which is of the essence of the religious system. Whether the negation be specific or discernible only as a resultant of the positive, its complementary role in the creation of the resources and the restrictions from which the religious thinker proceeds must be recognized.

Further, such an individual will be limited by that from which he proceeds unless he is sufficiently aware of the thought and traditions which lie beyond his own resources. It is this awareness or lack of it which marks him as being either a citizen of his time, enriched by his tradition, or only a man of his tradition who is restricted by it. It is only when he is fully cognizant of the resources and insights which have developed ouside his own heritage that he is prepared to articulate that which is his own in a manner meaningful to others. It is only then that he can be in a position to begin to understand the limitations and potentialities of that from which he comes and now considers to be his own.

It is in the meeting of the familiar with the different that new insights most often arise. It is at this point that the religious thinker must be ready to follow out the consequences of his participation in the confrontation between his view and the thought of others. There must be an anxiety which leads him to seek to develop methods of procedure and avenues of communication whereby the different becomes better known and the familiar more fully understood.

The sensitive theologian will be especially conscious of the tensions which must inevitably be present when the familiar and the different are in confrontation. There are tensions which are soon dispelled as the unknown becomes known. There are tensions which persist because they stem from legitimate differences inherent in the systems of belief being considered. And there are tensions which are productive because they serve to heighten insight and to excite new thought because of the healthy strain they place upon that which is traditional and cherished. The tension accompanying religious faith held in the midst of challenge from outside often has proved, throughout the history of religion, to be more fruitful than destructive.

Thus it is that the religious thinker of the present day will proceed from the universal implications of his own religion to the task which that universality demands of him. It will take him into areas which he has not known, and demand that he learn facts before he creates theories. It will demand a sensitivity to the currents of thought of his own time whether they be designated religious or not. It will require that this sensitivity and its resulting perceptivity be directed toward elements and traditions of human thought and conduct which lie historically outside one's own tradition. Above all, it will impose upon the religious seeker who endeavors to serve his faith in his own time tensions which will bear fruit only because they are tensions attended by perplexity, doubt, and intellectual and spiritual pain.

2

The religious requirements of our time are not necessarily different in essence from those of previous periods in history. They may differ in degree of intensity, in relationship to that which is central at one period and peripheral in another, or in the insistence with which they demand attention. Differences between eras of history often originate from the peculiar meeting of separate events, developments, and demands. Particular matters are made more pertinent for one age than for another because of the flux of the total culture. In the area of intellectual endeavor associated with theology and philosophy, the fundamental question remains the same. These disciplines are concerned with the basic problem of the meaning of existence, and the problem itself does not change. What changes is the amount and growth of knowledge about the nature and structure of elements and forms of human and material existence. This growth in understanding of the human being and his surrounding environment is accompanied by changes in the many elements which collectively constitute the current social structure and the culture of a given time and place; the ultimate problem remains the same.

The contemporary problems which confront religion are well-known to all who are alive to the world they live in. Religion in its higher forms has often been faced with opposing systems of belief and with doubt. The confusions which today beset religion are in large degree the result of either religious doubt, which takes the generally quiet form of agnosticism or indifference, or of more active atheism expressed in a philosophy, in literature, or in political-economic movements. These obviously result, in part, from the inadequacy of religion, the failure of religion to express its values in terms which have pertinence and meaning to the problems which man is facing. This is not to maintain that when a particular system of religious belief and practice is not accepted by all men, the religion is totally at fault. Truth is not established by popular acceptance. It is dependent upon precise formulation and clear enunciation as well as upon its intrinsic value.

Opposition to religion, which takes the forms we have suggested, may also be traced to the preoccupation of man with matters essential to life but separate, in the understanding of many, from the nature of religion and its universal concerns. For the religious man who is sensitive to the dimensions of religion, such a separation is either impossible or is made at peril to his faith and its integrity. Despite the interest in religion apparent among so many, there is an indifference to religion because of its isolation from large areas of human life and activity. The claims which the major religions make for the relevance of their teachings in these areas are dismissed by many. This results in confusion as to the nature of religion itself, as well as in obscuring its significance in important spheres of life.

This current confusion and the failure of religion to achieve its goals are indicative, in part, either of the inadequacy of the traditional presuppositions and values of the established religions or of the present unsuitability of methods of expressing and propagating them. In later chapters we shall consider the four leading religions of the world today in an attempt to understand their essential themes and potential relevance to the future of man and his culture. It will be apparent immediately that, if the religious problem today is primarily one of presentation, the future adequacy of the fundamental beliefs of the religions will be difficult to determine. While it is a truism that religion has greater depths of value than can be seen simply from its formalized and theoretical expressions, it is an arduous task to discover these merits if the traditional and accepted expressions of them tend to obscure their worth.

If it is a question of the truth of present religious belief and teaching on the part of the leading religions, it has long since been discovered that such truth is not established easily if at all. Argument which follows the rules of logic and self-consistency has not removed all religious doubt. Even the authenticated experience and testimony of reliable and trusted witnesses who have "tried" a religion, have not always served to convince others as to the independent and universal truth and value of the religion. We shall have to content ourselves by simply calling attention to the essential values and themes which appear to be present, recognizing that in the final analysis they are to be substantiated only partly by their intellectual cogency and partly by their contributions to a meaningful and integrated life among their adherents.

It is this fact which should cause us to refrain from expecting that any one religion will be accepted universally if it is somehow established to be founded upon ultimate truth. Philosophers have speculated throughout history concerning the final criteria for the verification of truth. Men have learned by experience that truth possesses both a relative and an absolute character, wherein its assumed absolute element is constantly being challenged by those who do not accept the assumption. And once it is suggested or allowed that a truth may in any sense be relative, that truth is usually rejected because of the common belief that truth is absolute. All of this suggests that to expect a particular religion to ever be accepted fully by mankind is to misunderstand the nature of religion.

To be dynamic, religion must be in tension and in suspense. At the same time that a religion fulfills its function of contributing to the integration of the individual—to what, rightly understood, may be termed a healthy-mindedness—it must be allowed to enter into serious dialogue with doubt and opposition. When the tension which accompanies such conversation is absent, religion often becomes sterile and ceases to meet its obligation to its adherents and their society. The contribution of religion to mankind tends, in such instances, at most to simply support the accepted and traditional. It does not aid man in the constant struggle to integrate the new with the old. As a result man and society are in confusion, and religion is in decline.

3

The situation of the present day is also a reflection of the confusion of individual men and women. It has been created by the totality of world society which, because of that confusion, has not been receptive to the new demands that are placed upon all human groupings and their cultures. While it is obvious that a culture molds the individuals subjected to it, generations of individual men and women create, shape, and change culture. The process is slow, and the alterations in most instances are separately minute. However, in their total impact over a span of time, each variation or modification does its part in the process of cultural change. The condition which we face is a result of the inability or refusal of responsible individuals to play this important role in their separate cultures. And now that each separate culture is being brought into a significant relationship with all other cultures, the support and guidance of responsible cultural leaders is of the greatest urgency.

We are, therefore, the recipients of a mandate which can be ignored only at our own peril. It is a mandate for new religious thinking, for the application of our religious and intellectual powers to the problems of our time. There are those who will ask if this is not what religious thinkers have done in all ages, and who will see in our suggestion simply a call to the continuation of the theological endeavor of the past. To the degree that this is a matter inherent in the theological and philosophical task of every age, they are correct. However, the import of the present mandate will be missed if it is not recognized that something more is required than what theology and philosophy have attempted and accomplished in previous periods.

We have said that there is now a mandate for *new* religious thinking. This will lead to misunderstanding and opposition. It will appear to many religious people that they are being requested to give up the values and the forms of their present religious faith, and that the definite assertion is being made that current religious belief is false and not valuable for the present. It is essential that we have clearly in mind what is meant when we speak of *new* religious thinking and the requirement for it which now exists.

This does not mean the dismissal of all that is now possessed. It involves neither the deliberate rejection of the presuppositions which are central to a specific religion nor the abandonment of the traditional cultic forms and social structures. Constructive approaches to new situations must always proceed with the recognition that beliefs and actions which have demonstrated their value in the past are not to be summarily abandoned. Such elements have not persisted simply because they were once found to be true or useful; they are not maintained only because they are part of the inherited tradition of a people and their culture. Rather, they have continued because in each successively new generation they have contributed to a meaningful understanding of life for great numbers of people.

The new religious thinking will obviously, and of necessity, be based upon the old. It will be required that the old be retained to the degree that it is a carrier of the truth which men continue to seek to understand more fully. It will be a tragic mistake if it is not remembered that the religious thought of previous human history is much more than the vehicle whereby humanity has preserved the revealed and discovered truths of the past. Rightly understood it is not a static conveyor of ancient thought. It is proper to say that religion has a future, because the religious beliefs and insights of humanity have demonstrated themselves to be pertinent in successive and changing periods of history.

Therefore, what we have termed the *new* will in large measure be created by a reinvigoration of the religious traditions and beliefs of the past and the present. It will be based not only upon what has gone before, it will continue it and carry it forward. The problem of the theological task which we face will be to make more explicit the values of the beliefs which are the heritage of the different religious cultures of today. It is demanded that they be conveyed in terms and by methods which are appropriate to the present and the developing future. And, while we cannot know that future, it is our conviction that the present intellectual, cultural, and political-economic condition of world society does give us insight into what is demanded of the leading religions. If religion, as it is now known, is to be viable to the generations of mankind who will live in the future, whatever it may be, these demands must be confronted. We hope by our subsequent consideration of these religions to establish that the demands of our time and the immediate future are not demands which will pervert the religions. We believe that if they confront contemporary men and their societies, without the essential theological-philosophical themes which have given them their strength and relevance in the past being discounted in any way, the great religious traditions will discover resources for the meeting of their responsibilities.

The foregoing is but one aspect of the two-fold responsibility which the mandate of the present day places upon the religious thinker. The other is perhaps more difficult, certainly potentially more dangerous, to the inherited religious values which at present sustain the major religions of the world. It is the requirement which

we have already suggested and which shall be a major thesis underlying our discussion, namely, that at the same time the religious
thinkers of the world seek to apply the values of their inheritance
to the problems of today, they are under the further mandate to
break the bonds which the accustomed provincialism of their religious thought has imposed upon them. The universality of both
the claims and potential contributions of their religion will remain
dormant and unrecognized until they do so. And, above all, they
must diligently seek to make these claims and to materialize these
contributions with an awareness, and in a language, commensurate
with the scope of the universal endeavor upon which they are required to embark.

II
The
Christian
Message

The two thousand years of Christian history have witnessed a long process of theological speculation and development. Like all such phenomena of human life, this thought and concern has been related to a past which preceded it. In the case of Christian theology, the two dominant and most influential sources for its own structure and development were the specifically religious Jewish ethos which had surrounded the founding of Christianity and the broad cultural atmosphere of Hellenism. The first was primary in setting the theological stage by bequeathing an ethical monotheism, while the latter dominated the expression of the developing theology by its contribution of categories of thought associated with the Greek intellectual influence upon the larger part of the developed western world. As the leading force in the development and expression of the mind-set of western thinking from early in the Christian era, Christian theology has served as the primary vehicle for the continued leading influence in the West of the Hebraic, or Semitic, religious understanding of human existence. Throughout much of western history, by its employment of the legacy of Greek philosophy, it has contributed also to the making of the western philosophic understanding of the universe.

As the almost absolute monarch of western thought for more than a thousand years, Christian theology not only created and gave form to western religious and philosophical thinking but also served as the primary arbiter in the determination of the social structure of those centuries. Here, again, it was the inheritor of a political and social order which had preceded it and which had been dominant at the time of the rise of Christianity. By a subtle

process, both as an institutional religion and as a system of theological thought, Christianity came to be identified in large part
with the Roman social and political order. And, with the disappearance of that order as a formal force in the areas of its former
power, Christianity served as the continuer of much that had been
Roman in the last days of the empire.

However, the Hebraic-Greek-Roman legacy did not complete the
cluster of forces which served to shape the thought-world and social
structure of the centuries when Christianity reigned supreme in the
western world. There were also the less noticeable influences which
came from the many small and relatively unimportant political and
cultural areas of Europe and the Near East. Many and varied
within themselves, they had been participants in the total Graeco-
Roman world. In a measure they had lost their identity in that
environment; nevertheless, each had its own contribution to make
to its own future and the total future of the West. The semi-
Asiatic peoples of the eastern Mediterranean, the theologically
acute thinkers of northern Africa, the Germanic peoples of the
north, the later peasantry of Europe—these and others like them
made contributions to the unified whole which emerged into the
form of Christian theology and Christian faith.

A discussion of Christian theology, therefore, is required to proceed on the assumption that the variety of contributing sources to
Christian thought and practice is definitely recognized. Even a brief
consideration of such a broad phenomenon as a leading religion
and its complex thought must not proceed as if the matter under
discussion is singular in its source and uniform in its nature. A
society, a culture, a religion, a theology, a philosophy—each are of
such complex nature in origin that detailed study of even their most
primary sources would be almost never ending.

The problem is complicated by the question of what the primary
forces are in the creation or emergence of such phenomena. Can
these be precisely discerned and, once identified, can they be adequately portrayed? This and related problems will raise difficulties
for us in our consideration of each of the leading systems of religious thought in the contemporary world. We shall be forced to
content ourselves by calling attention to the large number and wide
variety of contributing factors in the origin of a complex religion,

as well as insisting that note be taken that a religion and its thought system also rise out of an individual and corporate experience which is primary in significance.

This latter suggestion is made because it would appear that something is missed in a discussion of religion which omits an appreciation of the factor of religious experience itself. The nature of religious experience is complex and to a large extent elusive. The difficulty in making a satisfactory definition of religion often stems from the ineffable nature of the experience which lies behind the religious expression. Definitions well-known to the scholar aid in guiding the study of religion, but they do not succeed in even a preliminary exploration of the range and dynamic of the initial impulse to religiosity within man, nor of the continuing motivation and inspiration it gives. Behind the outward sociological, cultic, and theological expressions of a religion, there lies the individual and collective religious experience which is the primary reason for the existence of the religion. Hidden within religious beliefs and language there is the memory of an experience, and the dynamic of that event continues to create new attempts to articulate the meaning of the encounter between man and the Divine.

Christianity may rightly be said to have been the collective religious expression of the western world for the major portion of the past two thousand years. At some periods this position of supremacy has been unchallenged, while at other times it has been not only challenged but reduced markedly. In some instances, movements which possessed within themselves power to dispute some of the basic foundations of Christianity have been absorbed into the Christian sphere and used to support it. Philosophies, political ideologies, economic theories, and social systems have had their tensions, expressed their oppositions, and often made their adjustments to Christianity.

However, such a process of social-cultural-religious adjustment is not limited to those elements other than religion. Religion, too, is required to reconcile itself with its partners in the total cultural environment. The end result is that each of the elements of the whole tends to merge together to the point where its distinctiveness is lost and its identity obscured. Despite non- or anti-religious elements within the civilization, and notwithstanding protests against aspects of the society by the religion, the civilization and the religion all too easily come to be considered as one, often correctly so. In the case of Christianity and the West, the identification has been almost absolute in periods such as the High Middle Ages when Christianity appeared to be the all-inclusive and unchallenged arbiter of western civilization. At present the identification is made with hesitancy, and with the awareness that it is at best only a figure of speech, a misleading one at that. Adequate analysis of either time may prove the homogeneity to be more imagined than actual, but even the conception has served to shape the West's understanding of itself and its religion.

In the days of its initial migration beyond the boundaries of Palestine, the earliest theological expressions of Christianity gave ready recognition to the relationship of the new religion with its Jewish past. The founder of the new faith and the messenger of the new Gospel was understood by his followers to be humanly in the line of the greatest personage in the Jewish past. He was also, and far more importantly, conceived to be inherently related to the God of the Hebrew Covenant in a manner which placed him in a different category from all other men. He was the Divine, not as some others had been held to be in the Graeco-Roman world and elsewhere because of their attainments or their high political-religious position. Jesus was the Christ, the Divine Son sent into the world to bring men the grace of God and thereby the gift of salvation. And this God of Grace is the God who had been proclaimed by Jewish ethical monotheism for centuries. As that God incarnate in human history, Jesus appeared as the fulfilment of the Jewish religious hope, and he preached his message in the midst of the Jewish religious tradition.

Once embarked upon its mission to areas outside that tradition, Christianity came into direct contact with the second major factor in its future theological development. In the necessary endeavor to express its theological foundation, early Christianity found itself forced to state its teaching in both the language and the categories of thought which were familiar to its auditors. In so doing Christianity brought about a union of the Semitic core of its religious message with the Hellenistic metaphysical-philosophical-religious world-view. Since that time, these two have served together to constitute the warp and woof of Christian theology.

Through the centuries of theological speculation, debate, and development, the Semitic heritage of the Christian faith has been made meaningful to Christian adherents by means of words coined within the philosophic tradition ancient to Athens and developed in the Greek and Roman centers of the Mediterranean world. In the periods of intense theological and intellectual flowering, subsequent Christian thinkers forged their thought in the Latin which that world had bequeathed. And, as that language served as the common intellectual medium of the developing western Christian culture, so, too, the ancient philosophy was the unifying intellectual agency. The religious experience of Palestine and the philosophical insights of Greece combined with the political genius of Rome to create the western Christian civilization of Europe.

We have suggested earlier that the present condition of religion in the western world does not possess the vital directing importance in the realms of thought, culture, and society that it once did. This has been done with full consciousness of the extreme difficulty of accurately weighing the power and force of religion in a pluralistic society such as now exists in the West. Even in times and areas where a particular Christian religious organization is by and large unchallenged by any other organized religious or secular group, such supremacy does not necessarily mean that the religious impact upon the society is determinative. In Western history Christianity frequently has lost its vitality and has abdicated from its essential religious responsibilities in order to maintain its formal standing in the society.

However, it is not of the nature of Christianity to remain willingly in such a position for long. Included in its Hebrew heritage of ethical monotheism was the prophetic tradition inherent in such a conception of the Divine. This legacy has caused the Christian faith to abandon security and drop complacency before and it will no doubt do so again. Like all living religions, Christianity is related to the civilization which surrounds it. It is inextricably involved in the values and faults, the problems and hopes, which are inevitably common to a religion and the environment around it. Since western civilization is concerned with its own survival and, more importantly, with the contribution of the values it holds most precious to the world civilization which is emerging, a Christianity which will consider itself removed from such concerns will not be a religion worth retaining, nor will it be the dynamic Christianity which the West has known in important periods of the past. It is difficult to imagine that either the institutional Christianity or the Christian theology of today will not accept the challenge that their present circumstance and past history place before them.

1

After briefly questioning whether the Gospel was so uniquely Jewish in nature that it might be restricted to Judaism both in its outreach and its form, the early Christian faith recognized its commission to be one which demanded that it break out beyond the confines of the religious ethos which had surrounded its birth. With that acknowledgment, Christianity was compelled to enter into communication with a religious and philosophical world which was varied in composition, the product of many diverse peoples and cultures, all of which had been brought together into the larger whole of the Hellenistic world-view by the unifying Roman political power. Collectively these groups had created a religious opinion which gave a basic unity of religious thought and practice within the variety of elements which contributed to the Hellenistic world.[1]

Students of early Christian history have been intrigued by the relationship between Christianity and the other religions of the time. It would appear that the new religion was at one with many of its fellows in certain respects.[2] Primary among these was the proclamation that immortality was available to those who adopt the faith. A divine savior had appeared who by his triumph over human death had bestowed eternal life upon those men and women who placed their trust in him. Further, this great gift to mankind was to be obtained through participation in religious acts limited to those who freely declared themselves desirous of membership within the group. A personal decision was involved. Receipt of this salvation was not the result of status of birth nor membership in a political community. Most important of all, the divine savior had himself experienced death in order to conquer it for man.

It is not necessary for our purpose to give a detailed account of the prevalent religious thought of the time, nor do we need to exhaustively and precisely cite the similarities and differences between Christianity and the other religions.[3] Yet it is important that we be aware that Christianity was not *totally* different in its proclamation nor in its acts of worship. The claims of Christianity were different to a large degree in their emphasis and in their total and exclusive unified demand upon men. With the later development of Christian theological thinking, the statement of that demand and the uniqueness of the total Gospel were made more clear. However unique the Christian belief may have been in essence, and in the minds of its earliest adherents, that unparalleled nature was not clear at first to the people of the Graeco-Roman world. For this reason the new religion was required to put forth its claims of divine origin and human relevance with vigor, and with care that its expressions were meaningful in the religious and philosophic thought-world of the time.

The earliest centuries of Christian theology were marked by the attempt to state clearly the nature of Jesus, the Christian community or Church, and the means whereby the saving grace of God was given to members within the Church. In these and other matters the scholars and the leadership of the Church needed to justify the new religion as the authentic fulfilment of the truth adumbrated in Judaism, while demonstrating that it went beyond the Jewish religion in its authority and in its universal message to all men.

Theology thus became the primary means whereby the early Christian Church sought to establish itself within the intellectual community of the Graeco-Roman world. And, while a proper evaluation of Christian history would be likely to establish that Christianity at no time has achieved or maintained high place in western civilization primarily on the basis of its intellectual expression, it is important to note that the Church has at most times been greatly conscious of the importance of careful and coherent theological statements. The majority of men are won to a new religious understanding of life by a direct experience of the truth and value of the religion, an experience which involves the total being in an appreciation of itself and existence in a manner not fully comprehended previously. Cogent intellectual defenses of religious truth are of greater concern after the experience than before. Theology may aid in the conversion of the rare individual; more often it serves to aid in understanding what is believed and to convey intelligible thoughts about it.

From its earliest beginnings Christian theology has, therefore, expressed itself in a language and form which has been a part of the social and intellectual environment of the time. It sought to make clear to itself and to others the nature of the person of Christ by means of the recognized philosophical norms of scholarship. In so doing, theology was a prime factor in the rediscovery of learned thinkers of the past and in the continuing knowledge of their contributions. And, under the necessity of formulating a new system of thought with terms and concepts not always adequate for the task, Christian theologians in many instances were the creators and shapers of a new philosophy which, while theological and Christian in nature, was highly dependent upon the Graeco-Roman philosophy which was at its base.

Once Christianity had become known within the Mediterranean world, it was subject to attack from the intellectuals of the time. Where governmental authority saw in the new religion a divisive and uncooperative faction within the society, and other religions were conscious of another opponent to themselves, the scholar and thinker discerned a way of believing and acting that defied the common-sense understanding of existence and the universe. Greatly disillusioned themselves, by and large, with the accepted religious beliefs and practices of the time, they found in Christianity not only another foolish religious sect, but one which made unintelligible and indefensible pretensions to an absolute possession of eternal truth. Within its first few centuries the Christian faith demonstrated an ability to win adherents, and this the philosophers could understand as being the result of the ignorance and stupidity of men. However, Christianity also was willing and anxious to enter into a discussion of its teachings on grounds which were not totally different from those on which the philosopher operated. And while it would be erroneous to contend that early or later Christian theo-

logians did not appeal ultimately to a source of authority greater
than the human reason, or that they and their philosopher opponents acknowledged in all cases the propriety of each other's
reasoning even though disagreeing with the conclusions, yet it is
necessary to be aware that a type of conversation had begun between
theology and philosophy.[4]

From the earliest theological statements of Saint Paul and other
writers of the New Testament, the uses of philosophy by the Alex-
andrian theologians and others, the theological-philosophical controversies with non-Christain opponents, to the high attainment of
theological thought revealed in the writings of Augustine of Hippo
—in each case Christianity demonstrated itself to be a religion
which sought to express its beliefs in language commensurate with
the highest human intellect. The fact that these teachings were
firmly believed to be received from the one God of all existence,
coupled with the growing conviction that truths received from
divine revelation would not be different from any truths ascertained by the human intellect, impelled the Christian thinker to
enter into the fray of intellectual combat. All correct human
knowledge was ultimately dependent upon superhuman agency.
Truth was a gift from God. Error could be established when it was
held up to comparison with the specific divine revelation in Christ.
By his creation man had been endowed with the capacity for in-
telligence, and it was the duty of Christian theology to lead that
potential understanding of truth to the highest levels of which it
was capable.

Also, with the emergence within Christianity itself of intellectually able and concerned individuals, the need to formulate the essentials of the faith in forms acceptable to such minds became
inevitable. A prime example of this was in the matter of the nature
of Jesus. The many preachers of the Christian message came from
different backgrounds and with varied understandings of such per-
plexing and complicated statements as that Jesus was the Son of
God, and was one with God. In their zeal to win others and to
further the allegiance of those already within the Church, they often
presented a Christ who did not correspond with the general understanding of the majority of Christian adherents. In many instances
these deviations became well established among Christians in cer-

tain areas, and they were upheld often by theological champions of great brilliance. Others saw in such positions concerning Christ elements which would either detract from his ultimate divinity and the efficacy of the salvation which he brought to man or would, they maintained, jeopardize the final and absolute unity and dignity of God. In such controversies it was necessary that dogmas be created which would win the religious and intellectual assent of the increasingly large and varied membership of the Church. And, in the establishment of these theological formulations, the overcoming of opponents was not to be done only on the basis of a demand for faithful acceptance of the majority opinion. It also involved an appeal to previous teachings of belief by respected earlier Christian authorities and the use of the most subtle and persuasive tools and categories of human reasoning. Theology was required to appeal to the authority of the past and to the criteria of the contemporary rules of human thought in establishing the definitive formulations of eternal truth which, it was held, was ultimately beyond time and the limitations of man's intellect.[5]

Christian theology was, therefore, dependent upon the divine revelation in Jesus Christ, the authority of the Apostles or early teachers of the faith, and the philosophical framework of western thought. In its basic teachings concerning God, Jesus Christ, the Church, man, salvation, and immortality, all three of these authorities had their place. Though the ultimate appeal was to the revelation in Christ, in each case the statement made was subject to human understanding and the philosophical ethos which shaped that understanding.

The high point of the interaction between theology and philosophy, of the dependence of theology upon the procedures and restrictions traditionally inherent in western philosophy, was reached in the scholastic theologians of the High Middle Ages. This is most clearly demonstrated in the system of thought developed by Saint Thomas Aquinas in the thirteenth century. By this time Christian thinkers of Europe had come to have a knowledge of Greek philosophers of antiquity to a degree not possessed in the immediately preceding centuries. Though this knowledge was not always correct, it did, nevertheless, reveal to medieval theologians a possible precise structure for the statement of the essentials of Christian theology.[6] It also opened the minds of the theologians of the period to philosophical problems they had previously, often unknowingly, averted or ignored. The result was both a flowering of theological production and attainment and a feeble but increasingly important rebirth of philosophy as a possible independent discipline of human intellectual endeavor in the West. The rise to full stature of rational thought by man, independent of divine revelation, remained as yet for the future, but the initial steps had been made for the eventual radical gulf between theology and philosophy typical of today. In the brilliant use of a type of procedure and construction of thought primarily associated with philosophy, theology had acknowledged its inherent relationship with the processes of human thought.[7]

The apparently complete success of Christianity in establishing itself as the religion of the western world, had resulted in the turning of theological thought inward upon itself and its own concerns. Even with the emergence of Islam as a direct and ever present threat to Christianity and European culture, intellectual controversy was between individual theologians and schools of theological thought. With the rise of Islam, and its demonstration of a high attainment of theological insight and presentation, Christian theology was once again called upon to present its claims against a strong opponent. Yet since the two religions did not, by and large, appeal to the same audience, nor engage in an intellectual or religious but rather a military struggle, Christian theology did not concern itself directly and vigorously with the necessity and opportunity afforded to it. Christianity, as it had been known for centuries in Europe was seemingly secure as the religion of the people, the director of the culture, and the arbiter of men's minds. Only a few of the leading theologians at most were conscious of the theological arguments of Islam, and they tended to dismiss them with short notice.[8]

Students of the Reformation of the sixteenth century are aware that there were many antecedents, contemporary causes, and theological principles involved in its beginnings and its course. Since we are concerned here with the general development of Christian theology we need mention only that the break within the larger unity of the Christian Church was political, economic, cultural, cultic, moralistic, pietistic, *et cetera,* as well as being theological. However, it was the occasion for a resurgence of theological activity. It had been preceded by a rapid growth of intellectual awakening and ferment in the century before and was accompanied by the results of the Renaissance, especially as revealed in the Humanism of intellectuals such as Erasmus. The theologians associated with Roman Catholicism in the struggle depended heavily upon such contributions, and the Protestant theologians were often more deeply in debt to the new "secular" intellectual insights than they realized.

The growing separation between various spheres and activities of life, revealing itself in Europe from the Middle Ages on, was indicative of a rising appreciation of the potentialities and capabilities of individual and collective man. It was also a repudiation of the exclusive claims of the Christian Church in the affairs of human life and thought. Where the Church had succeeded, with a few important exceptions, in establishing itself as the prime factor in European life, and theology had been the intellectual autocrat determining the forms and horizons of human thought, now these two in their united and in their separate functions were being vigorously challenged. The history of the subsequent centuries, and the problems of our time, are the record and inheritance of the separation of the Christian religion from the secular world of man's activities and thoughts. The fault, if there be one, is not limited to either side of the separation. Nor is it necessarily to be regretted that it occurred. The tragedy lies in that, despite occasional valiant efforts, neither of the two new opponents have succeeded in establishing and maintaining the needed productive conversation and relationship with each other.

The intellectual activity of the last centuries has revealed an intense concern that all knowledge be integrated in order to relate, not separate, the various demands upon modern man, to unify and not divide, to complement and not exclude, and above all, to contribute to man's wholeness and integrity, not to be destructive of his inherent need for coherent correlation between experience and understanding. The gulf between various types of intellectual activity has arisen not so much from a difference in aim of ultimate attainment as from divergence concerning acceptable methods of procedure and norms of authority. Since the loss of what was thought by many to be the ultimate synthesis of the Middle Ages, Christianity and western culture as a whole have been confronted by a confusion which has weakened the West's attempts to use the strength that the dissolution of the supposed synthesis has produced.

This confusion was brought most forcefully to the fore by the radical theological division which was manifest in the Reformation. It was furthered by the continued influence of the Renaissance; by the strength of Humanism; the contributions of the Enlightenment; the emergence of new political, economic, and social forms; and in the last decades by the almost unchallenged supremacy of science and its resulting technology. Each of these in its own way has proved to be a benefactor to man, yet each has contributed to the religious and intellectual disunity which plagues western man. It is of little avail to point to the value of conflicting systems of method and thought in stimulating constructive progress. Our knowledge that iron clad uniformity is productive of sterility and antithetic to worthwhile development, cannot be used as a defensible argument for the alternative of confusion which is debilitating to the human personality and the collective good. On the other hand, the irresistible desire to eradicate the confusion cannot be made the excuse for the creation of a uniformity which we know is destructive of the values of individuality both personally and socially.

The history of theology and philosophy during the recent centuries has been the continued attempt to confront this dilemma successfully. Few thinkers sensitive to the enormity of the problem and the depths of the human spirit have suggested the absolute uniformity which is feared by many men in the western heritage. Those that have put forth systems of thought which would demand unqualified unanimity of all men, have gained a measure of wide acceptance only when their thought was supported and expressed through force of a political nature. And those theologians and philosophers who have sought a unifying and cohesive super-system of thought, which would allow the maintenance of variety within a larger homogeneity, have not been able to overcome the disintegrative forces arising from the encouraged and permitted variety. The present resources for the attainment of religious belief and

intellectual insight which will enable man to possess even a mini-
mum of integration between his environment and his total spiritual-
intellectual-physical self, are not at the moment discernible to the
majority of men. Whether they will be in the future depends greatly
upon the theological sensitivity and activity of the present and next
generation of Christian theologians.

2

The basic themes of Christian theology will generally be known
to the reader of these pages. However, it is essential that we have
firmly in mind the elements which constitute the central core and
recurring themes of the Christian theological enterprise. As a body
of religious belief and commitment, as a formulation of intellectual
presuppositions, and as an expression of the religious experience
of individuals and the Christian community, theology has had its
foundations rooted in a set of primary affirmations which are
essentially religious, not philosophic, in character. The majority of
the Church have denied the Christianity of any constructions upon
this foundation which have not remained essentially in conformity
with the inherent structure of the elements in the foundation. And
any erections upon the basic substructure which have been primarily philosophical in nature have ceased to be theological if and
when they have allowed the human intellectual process to become
dominant over the essential cornerstone of divine revelation. In
the task that lies before it, Christian theology will find much of its
strength, and much of its problem, arising out of its inherent need
to remain true to these themes that have been integral to it throughout its history.

The complexity of a system of religious belief, even the most
primitive, arises out of the fact that each element within the system
is related closely to all other elements. One factor may be considered to be primary, but even that primacy is maintained by the
constant support of secondary elements which are absolutely essential in themselves. In a monotheism, for example, although the
Divine is the primary element and all other elements are derivative,
yet even the resultant elements are decisive in the religious and
theological understanding of God. For Christianity the belief in

the one God is absolutely primary, but that belief receives its content and is made meaningful religiously by further beliefs which go beyond the primary assertion itself.

Christian theology is the result of the religious experience which centers around the figure of Jesus the Christ. It is first and foremost a personal commitment to the person of Christ and only secondarily, though essentially, related to his actions or teachings. Any attempt on the part of a theologian or religious thinker to lessen the central importance of Christ as *the* Person, and to overshadow this element by his teachings or actions, has resulted in a departure from the orthodox understanding of Christianity. He is at the center of the early Gospel message and of the sophisticated theological systems of later times. Nevertheless, the person of Christ is not comprehended as an object of religious faith or as a matter of intellectual belief without the aid and support of the actions attributed to him and the teachings associated with his earthly ministry.

The Christian religious experience is grounded in the long history of religious experience and belief associated with the Hebrew people. Central to this heritage was the conception of ethical monotheism which we have cited as the Semitic legacy which has remained essential to Christian thought from the beginning. The Divine was held to be one, a unity which is the creator of the existence known and experienced by man. And this God is known to man primarily through history, in which It acts in a manner commensurate with Its own inherent standards. The fact that God is a God of standards is revealed in the nature of the demands placed upon man through his relationship with the Divine. God communicates with men through various means in which it is made known to man that there are those actions and thoughts which are proper and those which are not. The Divine is concerned that men recognize each situation in human life as one filled with potentiality for good and evil and that the outcome of any event is dependent in large part upon man's response to the potentiality.

The Hebrew heritage for Christianity was, thus, one in which a divine Being was held to exist both as the creator of material existence and the bestower of norms of human action and thought. There is that which is proper and not proper to each eventuality of existence, and the propriety or lack of it is determined by the God who has created all evistence. The Divine has created man and his environment, as well as setting up the proper manner in which man is to exist in his surroundings and his relationships with his fellow men. There is an ethical path for man to follow, and this path is made known to man by a God who acts in history to make Himself known. The vivid consciousness on the part of the Jewish people of the activity of God in their own history, and the history of the world, was a dynamic testament of the impact which this divine activity had made upon them.

It was in the appearance among men of the person of Jesus Christ that the divine activity in history was made most manifest. It was the early Christian conviction that God had acted decisively to make His will and His love toward men finally and conclusively known to men by placing His Son in the world. This conviction has remained central to Christian preaching and Christian theology since that time. Since Jesus of Nazareth was not only a man like other men who had been selected by God as a messenger, but was a man unlike other men because he was *the* Son of God, commitment to him was at the same time commitment to God. Jesus was the Christ, the Son of the living God present among men. Therefore, all that he taught and all that he did were the teachings and the actions of God. They were important not primarily in themselves as such, but because of the Person who said and did them.

The foregoing was inevitably the source of much intellectual perplexity in the early centuries of theological activity. For the Church as a whole the problems raised by the beliefs concerning the nature of Christ were settled in the important Christological controversies, waged particularly in the fourth and fifth centuries. For some groups of Christians the intellectual problem has continued, and their attempts to solve it have often taken them far from orthodox Christianity.[9] The point to be noted, however, is that any constructive attempt to bring Christian thought into a more decisive encounter with human problems in any age, present or future, will of necessity have to give allowance to the primacy of the place of Jesus Christ in the Christian religious commitment and its theological expression. It is in this matter of the incarnation of God in history in the Person of Jesus Christ that Christianity will perhaps always be a "scandal" to the human intellect. If so, theological thought can only continue to seek by every legitimate means to make that "absurdity" more clearly the key to the divine-human solution of man's problems in every age.

Historians of Christian thought have been greatly interested in the historic roots of the Christian emphasis upon man's low estate and the need for divine intervention to assure man's restoration to an original or correct relationship with God. The Hebraic conception of the early Fall of man from a state where he was unaware of evil to both awareness of it and a participant in it, obviously serves as one basis for the conviction that man, by disobedience to the divine will, had brought separation from God upon himself. The constant refrains of the Old Testament concerning God's love for man and man's perversity were further background for the Christian teaching that only God's love, and man's faith in that love, could bring about the immortality that was originally man's nature and had continued to be his hope. However, the growing Christian emphasis upon the essential distinction between the flesh and the soul of man was not primarily Hebraic. At this point the Hellenistic influence, partly Greek and partly traceable in origin to other eastern Mediterranean cultures and religions, made itself felt in early Christian interpretations of man and his predicament. The belief that man was composed of a spirit, or soul, which was in some fashion caught in the material body was rather general in much popular religious thought as well as in some more sophisticated philosophies.[10]

In the amalgamation of the Hebraic and the Hellenistic understandings of man, Christianity served to explain to man both his need and his ultimate hope. The need arose from his separation from God which was obviously a fact of earthly existence. The hope for man was to be found in the appearance of God among men to bring them back to Himself. In this both Christian orthodoxy and the later more liberal thought concerning man were in agreement. Whether man's return to the intended relationship with God was to be understood in the orthodox Christian sense, or whether it was to be understood as resulting from man's future full attainment of his potential powers under the guidance of God's grace, the result was the same. At least so thought the liberal thinkers.[11]

The latter understanding concerning man's predicament and his escape from it was to become more and more the liberal Christian position. Of course it was not uniformly contained in any one statement by those who considered themselves liberal; there have been wide variations of opinions within the general position. The importance of this liberal theological comprehension of man is that it reflected the growing trust of western civilization in the native ability of man to progress both materially and intellectually and, therefore, spiritually. These first two aspects of man were coming to be considered as the essential spheres of man's activity and his ultimate being. His essential soul or spirit would be in some measure the end product of his material and intellectual experience on earth. Through the last three centuries the increasingly liberal theological thought was involved more and more in a concern with the structuring of society as a means for the salvation of man in this fashion. The activities of God in Jesus Christ were not dismissed; they were understood in a different and more man-centered manner.

Man and his need were to be taken care of within the Christian Gospel by the application of the social teachings of Jesus to human society and to individual men. Jesus, the supreme Teacher, revealed to men the will of God; his Person possessed the love and compassion of God, and that love and compassion was to be continuingly exhibited in the world at the human level by men and women who themselves had learned of the graciousness of God through the teaching and example of Christ. Immortality, the fulfilment of man, was the end product of lives seeking to live in emulation of Christ. It was the result of ultimate truth discerned through dedicated lives and intellects sharpened to receive the full depths of the revelation in Christ.[12]

The foregoing concern with human betterment and Christlike living must not be identified only with the non-conservative or non-orthodox expressions of Christian thought. Theological conservatism or liberalism do not in themselves necessarily mean an opposition to or an identification with concern for the material and intellectual well-being of man. In the past both would claim such an interest, and currently the outstanding theological spokesmen for social justice and human material benefit are not necessarily those who put their trust in man's inherent capacities for good. The difference between the two groups, however, is that one does put primary emphasis upon man's incapacity and his need for special action by God, while the other, recognizing the ultimate dependence of man upon God, has a greater faith in man's resources to respond to God's grace in positive meaningful partnership with it in the achievement of a better, if not the proper, divine-human relationship.

The divergent emphases upon this recurring theme of Christian thought, namely, the nature of man and the means to his fulfilment, have marked much of Christian history especially in the more recent past. We have suggested that the more liberal view concerning man reflected a corresponding emphasis upon man's capabilities in the non-theological spheres of western life. It is to be wondered if this is not the crucial point of separation between most Christian theology and popular inherited religious belief on the one hand, and the intellectual scientific culture of the West on the other. While the latter may not consider man to be a creature endowed with an inherent tendency toward perfection in either knowledge or human relationships, yet it has demonstrated the capacity of man for a knowledge which can overcome, in part, many of the separate problems of the individual and society. Since these pressing matters were not conquered by the application of divinely revealed theological truths, but by the use of truths ascertained by the human intellect, it is not surprising that the relevancy of theology has been questioned by many in the present generation. The fact that the human intellect has by its attainments created more involved dangers, and potentially more devastating ones, is evidence that, while man's capabilities may be greater than much traditional theology has implied, his inherent tendency to self- and other-destruction may be exactly as Christianity has maintained.

Given the basic presuppositions of Christian thought as to the existence of God and the nature of man and his need, it follows that Christian theology has continually placed emphasis upon the imperative need of man for the grace of God mediated through the revelation of the Person of Christ. All men are under this need, and, without knowledge of the need and acceptance of the assurance in Christ that it can be overcome by the gracious gift of God, men will not receive the immortality which Christ brought. For this reason Christianity from its early beginnings has conceived itself as a universal religion. All men were held to be potential and rightful members of the Church. It was, therefore, the duty of the Church to carry the Christian message to them. In periods of greatest inner dynamic, often accompanied by political vitality in the surrounding environment, the Christian community engaged in missionary activity far beyond the previous geographical boundaries of its traditional strength.

It was this enterprise which brought Christianity into contact with its earliest opponents, both religious and secular. As the European and western awareness of the breadth of human society expanded, after the limitation of western horizons during so much of the Dark Ages, the religion of the West was faced with the duty to propagate its message actively and systematically. The supremacy of theology for so long a period in European history, and its identification with that area to the neglect of adjacent areas it had been so closely associated with in the earliest Christian centuries, had allowed theology to become provincial in its outlook and disdainful of foreign religious and intellectual thought. It insisted upon repeating in non-western cultural areas the essential themes of Christian faith in intellectual terms which were associated with its western, and specifically European, past.

The difficulty facing Christian theology in this regard must not be minimized. The problems confronting any attempt to express theological or philosophic thought in an ethos different from the one which has created and nurtured it are readily apparent. Christianity quickly learned the dangers and errors which arose from the attempts of well-meaning missionaries to put Christian belief in indigenous terms possessed of an apparently appropriate meaning but also a history of association with religious and philosophical thought which perverted the Christian intention. As a result, non-western converts to Christianity generally were required to adapt their thinking to the theological-philosophical categories of western thought which had become essential to Christian theological formulation. Deeply aware of the responsibility to carry the Christian message to all mankind, theology found itself incapable of separating itself from its provincial western past.[13] That it has so far not been able to do so is understandable; that it has made relatively little effort to do so is regrettable.

This problem is one which confronts any universal religious faith or system of thought. All religions have had their beginnings within a limited religious and cultural environment. If they have the opportunity to expand beyond the initial conditioning which formed them, they have to retain a large portion of their original message and self-understanding to escape losing their uniqueness. They cannot totally escape the thought-world of their birth without the possibility of the diminution or destruction of their reason for being. The basic themes, the source of their strength and the determining factors in their theological-philosophical structure, are elements which have their origin and primary meaning in the context of the initial thought-world of the religion. Subsequent elaboration or systematization of the thought of any religion always presents a peril to the original religious revelation or insight. When this process takes place within an ethos which is related to, or is not totally unlike the initial environment, the problem is difficult enough; when it must be undergone in the midst of highly developed and greatly foreign traditions of thought, it is well-nigh impossible to escape the loss of some of the original content.

However, the Christian religion and its theological expression is committed to the conviction that at all times and in all places the revelation in Christ must be made pertinent to men. The revelation itself is held to be so; the human expression of it through the Church and through theology must seek to make it so. The recurring themes of the Christian religion from its beginnings throughout its history are to be limited to the formulations of the past only if they are not of significance for the present. They are to be restricted to the intellectual traditions of the West only if they are not meaningful to men and women outside the West. God and His nature, Jesus Christ and his Person, man and the Christian revelation of his need and his hope—these essentials of Christianity and their derivatives—will not play the role in the life of mankind for which their adherents believe them intended if they do not escape their present restrictions. Christian theology has a duty, and that duty is of an imperative character which cannot be escaped.

3

The concerns of Christian theology during the past century and a half have been directed, in large measure, toward the problems which have resulted from the rise of science to its present status as the supreme factor in the life of western man. With this attainment on the part of science other matters have been lifted to a position of predominance as inevitable results of the power science affords to society and the authority which governs it. All social organization requires the presence of power to insure its continuation. The forms of society which tend to be required by a culture dominated by science, and which science produces in order to increase its efficiency, are social structures which increasingly tend to declare their independence of religion.

The result of this has been that western man's theological belief has not only been challenged by much of the scientific thought of the past decades, but man has also been forced to submit to an influence from his social organization which is often subtle and inescapable. The latter has always been a factor present in collective life; it is now especially disturbing because the theological bulwarks against it are themselves weakened.

The attempts of western religion to oppose, and then to adjust itself to, science are well known. In the nineteenth century this confrontation between Christianity and science was largely one wherein theologians were on the defensive concerning what they held to be the biblical truths which were the direct revelation of God.[14] With the accumulation of evidence which supported the growing scientific knowledge in the physical and biological areas of existence, theology was forced to come to terms with the new world of thought which was being produced. By and large this adjustment was in the form of a recognition by theology that religion was concerned primarily with the spiritual well-being of man and with his proper life in the world. Theological truths were concerned with God, Christ, man, and his salvation. Science was concerned with the structure of empirical existence.

However, such a separation of the areas of theology and science was a denial on the part of theology of what had previously been essential to its own understanding of itself and the claims of Christianity. Could theology abdicate a large share of its previous claims and continue to fulfil its duty to man? Was the Church or the individual Christian prepared to adjust from the traditional understanding of the nature of existence to the new scientific view without the aid and guidance of theology? The evidence of the past century strongly indicates that they were not so prepared. Theology may have been right in its recognition that its proper sphere was not precisely the same as science, but it failed in large measure to integrate science into the larger world view which theology continued to proclaim as essential to Christian belief and life. The relatively few theological thinkers who have been concerned with the total culture have had to work in an atmosphere of suspicion and distrust created by the Church and some of their theological colleagues. The fact that they are the theologians whose writings are read by today's intellectuals is indicative of their sensitivity to, and perception of, the fundamental problems of contemporary thinking men.

As a result of this inability of Christian theology to deal adequately with the new larger understanding of existence, either theologically or philosophically, Christian thinking has been centered more and more upon the essential themes of Christianity in order that a more meaningful understanding of them might be available to the Church in its confrontation with the modern world. The rise of scientific methods of literary and historical research has made available to scholars techniques which bring the biblical themes and the historical development of them into clearer focus. They were able to discern the historical setting of the books of the Old and New Testaments and gain insight into the religious development of Christianity's Hebrew heritage to a degree not known before. As a result, theological thought found itself without the support of the rigid biblicism which had come to be inherent, particularly in Protestant Christian thinking. Much of the theological liberalism of the late nineteenth and early twentieth centuries traced its thought to the results of the critical biblical scholarship of the time.[15]

However, with the rise of a more conservative theology, especially in Europe after the First World War, theologians and biblical scholars turned their attention more vigorously to the biblical themes which found their roots in the Old Testament and their full Christian expression in the New Testament. This new interest, known by the term Biblical Theology, has become in the middle of the twentieth century a primary factor in the theological expression of Christianity. It is a return to the Bible which calls upon Christian adherents and scholars to search for the biblical viewpoint, to seek to discover and articulate the biblical message to modern man. This is not a fundamentalism such as has been typical of some conservative American Protestant groups. Rather, it is a placing of emphasis upon the themes of the Bible as they are to be discovered in the Hebraic-Christian experience of God. It is an affirmation that the Bible must be understood in its own terms and within its own framework. It is the reassertion of the Christian claim that the Hebraic-Christian revelation of God is applicable to all times and conditions of men, with the added insistence that the revelation is best understood when seen in its historical context. On this basis, then, the Christian thinker will be able to apply the truths of Christianity to today. It is required of him that he not attempt to transfer totally the world-view of the historical setting of the Christian revelation. Rather, it is necessary that he apply himself to the discovery of the message contained within the revelation as expressed in the biblical environment and let that message speak for itself in the non-biblical context of the contemporary scene.[16]

The first half of the twentieth century has also witnessed a new and rapidly growing interest in the Christian community and its essential unity. Christians have become deeply conscious of the contradiction between the Church's message of unity in Christ and the division within the Church itself. Recognizing the historical reasons for the many institutional groupings of the Christian Church, Christian leaders have turned their attention to means to overcome those divisions now that the past causes no longer exist. Theologians and ministers, in particular, are more deeply aware of the meaning of the Church as a human institution with a divine commission from, and origin in, Christ. Theological emphasis upon the Church as *the* body of believers in Christ has laid the foundation for serious attempts to bring about a union in spirit and, where possible, in organization. This ecumenical movement has been primarily a Protestant concern and a Protestant endeavor, since that area of

Christendom has been most patently guilty of divisiveness. However, Roman Catholicism and the Orthodox Churches have also, each in their way, given evidence of greater desire to bring about a unity of all Christian believers as a fact of Christian life.

The theological concern with the nature of the Church, which has resulted from and supported the ecumenical movement, has produced a renewed interest in the common Christian heritage of both doctrine and worship. Protestant theologians have been brought back to an awareness of fundamental doctrines of Christianity which in some instances have been slighted, forgotten, or ignored by individual denominations. They have come to see that their own traditions and doctrinal emphases are part of a larger theological unity, and that, without the support of the whole of the Christian theological heritage, their own sectarianism is impoverished. It is not that the beliefs and doctrines of all Christian theological expressions are being, or are expected to be, accepted by all contemporary Christian groups; rather, it is that many are beginning to come to an appreciation of the richness, variety, and unity of the Christian religious experience. Those groups which have ignored, and even purposefully abolished, the more liturgical forms of worship, are beginning to awaken to the religious values which wisely used liturgy can give. Those groups which have placed their emphasis on rigid doctrine and/or formalism in worship, are rediscovering the merits of individual study and meditation upon the Christian revelation.

In company with these current concerns of the Church and theology, Christianity continues to express itself in the area of the broader social arena. The Social Gospel movement, particularly associated with liberal American Protestantism in the first decades of the twentieth century and also identified with some groups in British and Continental Protestantism, has continued to make itself felt. This, however, has been less a theological matter as such, and more a natural expression of the Christian concern for the physical and mental well-being of man. It has theological roots, of course, and its leading spokesmen in many instances are theologians. However, it is grounded primarily in the Christian concern for social justice rather than in the earlier liberal emphasis upon man's perfectability as a social being.

Both Roman Catholicism and Protestantism have sought, with varying success, to identify themselves with man's attempts to better his economic and social welfare. The Church has become more and more aware of the tendency to evil inherent in political, economic, and social power that is not constantly under judgment, both human and divine. The strong tendency for the institutional divisions of the Church and their leadership to become identified with the specific interests of their own membership, to the neglect of others in the society, has prevented the Church as a whole from taking the leadership in dealing with social questions, although it holds that to be its proper role in theory. Yet the Christian ministry in many areas is at the forefront of local social awareness and action. And in those areas and among those groups where this solicitude is lacking, both the ministry and laity are beginning to awaken to their Christian social responsibility. The foregoing does not mean that the Church is playing a dominant role in the approach to social questions in the western world, but it does mean that it is again coming to recognize more forcefully the social relevance of the Christian revelation.

This social awareness, which is becoming more central in the contemporary theological formulations of Christianity, is closely related to the whole problem of the relationship between Christianity and culture. As we suggested in our opening chapter, the mutual interaction between religion and culture is of paramount importance in any society and the basis of much of the world's present religious-secular difficulty. For Christianity, as all religions, the idea that any area of human life should, or rightfully can, be separated from religion is fundamentally not possible. True, there are areas of responsibility which must depend for their authority upon individuals and groups who are not necessarily identified with the Christian community, but the standards of performance and excellence achieved in these areas are of vital concern to Christianity. Religion which is limited to cultic act and metaphysical belief is not religion as Christianity has understood itself. In Christian history, those occasions when the Church has agreed to a division of powers have only occurred when other powers were sufficiently strong to force the separation.

Unfortunately in the past, and still too often in the present, the

Christian Church has conceived itself to be capable of absolute wisdom in areas in which it has no experience, and little understanding. As a result, its exercise of authority in the large cultural areas outside its competence has all too often been either a blight upon those areas or has caused a perversion of Christianity itself. Christian theologians and students of social problems are today coming to recognize their task as that of trying to develop the broad principles of Christian justice, ethical standards, and aesthetic taste which should apply within Christian culture. Christianity is developing a conception of itself as a partner in the creation and enrichment of culture. It is ceasing to insist that it be the sole locus of cultural authority and the autocrat of cultural expression.

The wide separation which now exists between western culture, particularly in the intellectual and aesthetic spheres, and the traditional religion of the West, is the product of many historic and recent causes. At present it manifests itself in the large amount of cultural activity which originates among people who are themselves not associated with the Christian Church, who, in fact, openly consider themselves in conflict with the institutional expression of Christianity. Excluding the important cultural leaders who are Jewish and in some instances separated from their own religion, the non-religious intellectual has failed to find in Christianity the religious experience and the intellectual-aesthetic stimulus and support he seeks. The fault, of course, does not lie only with Christianity. Such persons are often individualists by nature who find in their cultural creations and expressions the outlet for their individuality. They often express themselves most creatively in their revolt against the accepted and the traditional.

The complexity of the present situation, and the width of the gulf, is increased by the degree to which the Church, especially Protestantism, has in past decades evidenced little concern for the cultural arts. The great periods of Christian painting, sculpture, drama, music, and literature were the products of artists who found support in the Christian ethos which surrounded them. The Protestant environment has generally been one which discouraged such production. The cultural arts, therefore, have been forced to find their own support, and this support has come from areas which were either non-religious or anti-religious in character. Yet it is of the nature of the cultural arts that they find their most helpful nourishment in an atmosphere which, if not religious, does, nevertheless, possess some of the ingredients associated with formal religion. As a result, the arts have in many instances produced their own "religious" ethos in which they can express the aesthetic insights of contemporary man. From the lowest levels of artistic expression to the most sublime, they have sought to bring to modern man a sense of the emptiness of life, its potential fullness, and the aspirations of man. Painters in their attempts to plumb the depths of the visual experience of man have suggested both the disunity of experience and the possible final cohesiveness of all life. Perceptive musicians have done the same, and authors have portrayed man's confusion while seeking to convey man's dilemma in confrontation with life. For some there is a message of hope within their creations; for some there is only despair.[17]

That Roman Catholicism has continued to maintain a relationship with the cultural arts is to have been expected in the light of the Mediaeval and Renaissance traditions. However, even for Roman Catholicism this relationship has been greatly reduced by the widening gulf between Church and culture in the areas where Roman Catholicism has been the dominant Christian group. Individual members of the clergy and the laity have succeeded in expressing their aesthetic and intellectual insights within their Christian faith, but the fundamental cleavage between the culture which surrounds them and the religion to which they are committed is such that the two are far from being synthesized or collectively enriched. The separation remains within the society for the great body of mankind, and this lack of relationship creates a vacuum which entices into itself factors destructive of both society and Christianity.

It will be noted that the primary concerns of Christianity today, as an organized religion and Church and as an intellectual force in the life of the world, are those which, first of all, are centered in the Christian revelation and a more significant understanding of it for the life and faith of the Christian community. Secondly, they are related to the penetration of this revelation, in all its aspects, into the life and values of human society. Given the nature of religion, each of these concerns is necessary to the Christian institutional and theological enterprise. The attempt to ascertain more fully the import of the revelation of God in Christ will inevitably remain the central concern for Christian theology. It could not be otherwise. But it also is inevitable by the very nature of the Christian revelation that it will be demanded of theology not to remain restricted to the "theological" to the neglect of the equally important claims of the "non-theological." This is an unacceptable limitation to theology when there is full awareness of the breadth of the revelation which gives theology its *raison d'etre*. For the Christian religion there is, ultimately, nothing which is "non-theological."

In its unavoidable confrontation of the western culture, both its historic partner and opponent, Christianity has had available to it a common heritage vast in scope and meaning for both contestants. This shared resource has served each in their separate and joined developments; it has also furnished means for their antagonisms and their separation. In large measure this heritage remains the most productive avenue for the attempts of each to complement and enrich the other. In this aspect of its contemporary task Christian theology is required to seek to develop, by every power at its command, means of expression which, given the western inheritance, will make the Christian message pertinent to the problems of western man and his society.

But, the confrontation of Christianity with western culture is only one of the primary problems of relationship with culture which faces the Christian religion today and in the future. It is no longer possible to speak of culture in the provincial regional classifications which were permissible, and relatively correct, in past centuries. The one fact of human society, which along with science is the most important and inescapable of our age, is that regional cultures are now ceasing to exist. The degree of provincialism that they now exhibit is doomed to rapid dissolution. The separateness which has been characteristic of them, though always a qualified matter, is being bridged rapidly by means inevitably produced by the world-wide scientific revolution. Cultural isolation is no more possible than economic isolation, and the latter, under the stimulus of science, is bringing all societies into a vivid awareness of their mutual interdependence. Religion, which by nature is so closely related to culture, is caught in the same process of expansion, integration, and disintegration.

Because of its inherent commitment to present the Gospel to all mankind and its association with the migration of western civilization around the world in the past centuries, Christianity is now in meaningful confrontation with a variety of cultures, each of which is also contemporaneously being brought into relationship with the others as a result of the events of the past few centuries. Christianity is not only faced with the need to come into a vital relationship with its own historic culture, it is required to enter into a significant conversation with cultures distinctly foreign to it in content and expression.

The attempts on the part of Christian theological thinkers to express the Christian message and understanding of life in language which would have meaning to those outside the western cultural tradition, have been limited for the most part to the creation of techniques and forms for the statement of the Christian doctrine of salvation in Jesus Christ. This in itself is the primary first function of Christian theology in any conceivable situation. However, once the first attempt is made to fulfill this duty in any cultural context, theology is inescapably embarked upon an endeavor which is not limited to the more obviously religious message of salvation. The content of the Christian revelation of salvation is, as we have noted, one which extends to all areas and aspects of human life and society. That which at first glance might be thought to be limited to an affirmation of belief in a divine savior becomes, immediately it is done, an unlimited declaration of the relevance of the Person of that savior to all human thought and activity. For Christianity it cannot be otherwise.

The result has been that Christian activity in the non-western areas of the world has sought first to create a nucleus of Christian believers who would relate with others in their former religious heritage and be able on that basis to enlarge the local Christian community. However western Christians, with few exceptions, have not been equipped to proclaim the Christian message in its totality in a way which would arouse the interest of large numbers of people. They have had to rely on categories of religious and metaphysical thought which were western in development and meaning, and few non-westerners have discerned the significance of Christianity as a religious belief and a ground for action.

It is only in the past few decades that non-western Christians have begun to awaken sufficiently to the theological task which is now theirs. The duty they have is to seek to bring their new religious faith into significant relationship with their cultural heritage, a heritage which is not western nor historically Christian. In the fulfilment of their duty they will be faced not only with the necessity of expressing the historic Christian revelation in terms adequate for the new ethos in which Christianity now finds itself, they must also be deeply conscious of the need to make that proclamation in intellectual formulations which do not pervert nor dilute the revelation because of the demands of the culture. Their task is not unlike that which faced the early Christian thinkers who sought to proclaim in intellectual terms the revelation in Christ in the midst of Hellenistic thought. It is different, however, in that Christian theology through the centuries has become accustomed and, in fact, tied to categories of thought and means of expression which tend to make it rigid. Flexibility has not been totally lost but has become suspect among many within the Christian community.

The Christian Church is today a world-wide Church. The community of Christian believers is not limited to the West, nor is it composed only of those from one cultural tradition. The result is that the concerns of the institutional Church and of theology are not limited but are also world-wide. The present strong concern with the roots of the faith and their expression in the biblical setting, possesses the potential of supplying theological thought with resources for the articulation of the faith in meaningful terms to the contemporary world, a world which is neither western nor eastern, but rapidly becoming cosmopolitan. This cosmopolitanism is one which embraces all the functions, systems, beliefs, and expressions which combine to create a culture. It is the product of a growing interchange between societies and cultures which no longer can, or desire to, maintain themselves in exclusive isolation from each other. The concern of Christianity, as one of the religions within this emerging amalgam, is as wide as the whole of the separate parts. The duty of Christian theology to understand its task and express its affirmations, with due recognition of this cosmopolitanism, is imperative if the Christian Faith is to fulfill the role it claims for itself in the life of man and society.

NOTES

[1] S. Angus, *The Religious Quests of the Graeco-Roman World* (New York: Charles Scribner's Sons, 1929).

E. R. Bevan, *Later Greek Religion* (London: J. M. Dent & Sons, Ltd., 1927).

F. Aumont, *Les religions orientales dans le paganisme romain* (Paris: P. Geuthner, 1906).

H. Gressmann, *Die Orientalischen Religionen im Hellenistisch-römischen Zeitalter* (Berlin: Walter de Gruyter & Co., 1906).

G. Murray, *Five Stages of Greek Religion* (New York: Doubleday & Company, Inc., 1955).

[2] S. Angus, *The Environment of Early Christianity* (London: Gerald Duckwork & Co., Ltd., 1914).

E. R. Bevan, *Hellenism and Early Christianity* (London: George Allen & Unwin, Ltd., 1921).

R. Bultmann, *Primitive Christianity in its Contemporary Setting* (New York: Meridian Press, 1956).

C. Clemen, *Primitive Christianity and its Non-Jewish Sources*, trans. R. G. Nisbet (Edinburgh: T. &. T. Clark, 1912).

W. R. Halliday, *The Pagan Background of Early Christianity* (Liverpool: University Press, 1926).

E. Hatch, *The Influence of Greek Ideas on Christianity* (New York: Harper & Row, Publishers, 1956).

W. L. Knox, *Some Hellenistic Elements in Primitive Christianity* (London: H. Milford, 1944).

A. Loisy, *Les Mystères païens et le mystère Chrétien* (Paris: Émile Nourry, 1913).

A. D. Nock, "Early Gentile Christianity and its Hellenistic Background," *Essays on the Trinity and the Incarnation*, ed. by A. E. J. Rawlinson (London: Longmans, Green & Co., Ltd., 1928).

[3] B. M. Metzger, "Considerations of Methodology in the Study of the Mystery Religions and Early Christianity," *The Harvard Theological Review*, XLVIII, No. 1. A negative view concerning the relationship between Christianity and the religions of the Roman Empire. For example, on p. 20, ". . . if a judgment may be hazarded, the central doctrines and rites of the primitive Church appear to lack genetic community with those of antecedent and contemporary pagan cults." Reprinted by permission.

[4] The writings of the early Christian Apologists and the protests of their opponents reveal the conflict between pagan philosophy and Christian theology. The second century claim of Justin Martyr that Christianity is the truest of philosophies and Quintus Aurelius Symmachus' fourth century protest that "the heart of so great a mystery cannot ever be reached by following one road only" demonstrate the depth of the gulf between the two rivals.

[5] For the writings of early Christian theologians, the development of dogma, and the work of the great theological Councils, see:

A. Harnack, *History of Dogma*, trans. N. Buchanan, et. al., (7 vols.; London: Williams & Norgate, Ltd., 1896-1905).

A. Roberts and J. Donaldson, eds., *Ante-Nicene Christian Library* (25 vols.; Edinburgh: T. & T. Clark, 1867-73).

Philip Schaff, ed., *A Select Library of the Nicene and Post-Nicene Fathers of the Christian Church* (14 vols.; New York: Christian Literature Co., and Charles Scribner's Sons, 1886-1900).

[6] The considerable impact of Aristotle upon theological thought in the thirteenth century is noticeable particularly in the work of Albertus Magnus and Thomas Aquinas. Its most extreme result is seen in those thinkers (Averroists) who were greatly influenced by the Muslim commentator on Aristotle, Ibn Rushd (Averroes) and were condemned by the Church. See:

P. Mandonnet, *Siger de Barbant, et l'Averroïsme latin au XIII ème siècle,* (2nd ed., 2 vols., Louvain: Institut supérieur de philosophie de l'Université, 1908-1911).

[7] The Aristotelianism and Scholasticism of the thirteenth century may be said to have played both a negative and positive role in the development of the Renaissance of the following centuries. For example, Petrarch (1304-1374), the early Italian Humanist, revolted strongly against both, yet their rigidity and emphasis upon the thought and authority of antiquity served as an incentive to studies which were to produce results in marked contrast to their position.

[8] For the efforts of Christian theologians in the Middle Ages to understand and refute the theology of Islam, see:

Henri Pinard de la Boullaye, *L'Etude comparée des religions* (Paris: Gabriel Beauchesne, 1922), Vol. I.

[9] For some of the many works concerning early and recent Christological thought, see:

Gustaf Aulén, *Christus Victor* (New York: The Macmillan Company, 1931).

D. M. Baille, *God was in Christ* (New York: Charles Scribner's Sons, 1948).

Emile Brunner, *The Mediator,* trans. O. Wyon (London: Lutterworth, 1937).

A. M. Fairbairn, *The Place of Christ in Modern Theology* (New York: Charles Scribner's Sons, 1911).

H. M. Relton, *A Study in Christology* (London: S P C K, 1917).

W. A. Spurrier, *Guide to the Christian Faith* (New York: Charles Scribner's Sons, 1152), Appendix A.

[10] S. Mackenna, trans., *The Enneads* (2nd ed., London: Faker & Faker, Ltd., 1956).

W. R. Inge, *The Philosophy of Plotinus* (2 vols.; London: Longmans, Green & Co., Ltd., 1918). Perhaps the most developed and influential expression of this relationship is revealed in the thought of Plotinus, the great Neoplatonic philosopher of the third century.

[11] The so-called "Synergistic Controversy" concerning the role of man in his own salvation through the grace of God is not to be limited to the period immediately following the Protestant Reformation. The controversy is reflected in the arguments of Augustine and Pelagius in the fifth century, Flacius, Melanchthon, Calvin, and Arminius in the sixteenth century, Jansenists and Jesuits in the seventeenth century, the rise of theological liberalism in the nineteenth century, and the emergence of the twentieth century Protestant theology known as neo-Orthodoxy.

[12] From the theological endeavors of Schleiermacher early in the nineteenth century to the social gospel concerns of Rauschenbusch in the first decades of

the twentieth century, it is evident that an emphasis upon man's potentiality and his role in the creation of the Kingdom of God was present as seldom before, if ever, in Christian theology. A. Ritschl and A. Harnack in Germany, F. D. Maurice and J. Martineau in Great Britain, and W. E. Channing and W. A. Brown in the United States were a few of the seminal thinkers in the liberal theological development of the period.

[13] The attempt in the early years of the modern missionary period to equate the Chinese conception of Shang-ti with the Christian understanding of God, is a classic example of the complexities of the problem. For general discussions of the problem, see:

Raoul Allier, *La Psychologie de la Conversion chez les peuples non-civilisés* (Paris: Payot, 1925).

Daniel J. Fleming, *Contacts with Non-Christian Cultures* (New York: Doubleday & Co., Inc., 1923).

Lyndon Harries, "Bishop Lucas and The Masasi Experiment," *The International Review of Missions*, XXXIV (1945).

The Christian Life and Message in Relation to Non-Christian Systems of Thought and Life, The Jerusalem Series (vol. I; New York: International Missionary Council, 1928).

Hendrik Kraemer, *The Christian Message in a Non-Christian World* (New York: Harper & Row, Publishers, 1937).

G. E. Phillips, *The Old Testament in The World Church* (London: Lutterworth, 1942).

———, *The Transmission of The Faith* (London: Lutterworth, 1946).

H. P. Thompson, *Worship in Other Lands* (Westminster: S.P.G., 1933).

[14] It is difficult, if not impossible, to find the works of any theologian of the latter half of the nineteenth century which appear to the modern reader to compare favorably with the writings of those who approached the conflict between science and religion from the perspective of science. And, while contemporary theologians would not necessarily accept their positions, the attempts of philosophers such as Spencer and George John Romanes to reconcile Evolution and Religion are closer to the method of present-day theology than that of their theological opponents. See:

Herbert Spencer, *First Principles* (New York: Appleton-Century-Crofts, Inc., 1898).

George John Romanes, *A Candid Examination of Theism* (Boston: Houghton-Mifflin Company, 1878).

———, *Mental Evolution in Man* (New York: Appleton-Century-Crofts, Inc., 1893).

[15] For surveys of the development of critical biblical scholarship, see:

C. C. McCown, *The Search for The Real Jesus* (New York: Charles Scribner s Sons, 1940).

R. H. Pfeiffer, *Introduction to The Old Testament* (New York: Harper & Row, Publishers, 1941), Part I.

A. Schweitzer, *The Quest of the Historical Jesus,* trans. W. Montgomery (London: A. & C. Black, Ltd., 1910).

[16] Recent outstanding examples of this approach.

B. W. Anderson, *Understanding the Old Testament* (Englewood Cliffs, N. J.: Prentice-Hall, Inc., 1957).

H. C. Kee and F. W. Young, *Understanding the New Testament* (Englewood Cliffs, N. J.: Prentice-Hall, Inc., 1957).

[17] The growth of Protestant theological interest in the content and significance of the cultural arts has been especially noticeable since the Second World War in Europe and America. Witness in the United States the growing number of doctoral dissertations on the subject in recent years. For example:

P. Y. Roberts, Jr., "Theology and Imaginative Literature; An Essay in Literary Criticism from the Point of View of Christian Theology" (Ph.D. dissertation, University of Chicago, 1950).

N. A. Scott, Jr., *Rehearsals of Discomposure: Alienation and Reconciliation in Modern Literature: Franz Kafka, Ignazio Silone, D. H. Lawrence, and T. H. Eliot,* Ph. D. dissertation, Columbia University, 1949 (New York: Columbia University Press, 1952).

G. Vahanian, "Protestantism and the Arts" (Ph.D. dissertation, Princeton Theological Seminary, 1958).

III
The
Thought
of
Hinduism

The story of the development of thought and speculation in India is an account of human searching after understanding which parallels the few other great epics of philosophic endeavor in the world's history. In its earliest stages it ranks with the achievements of Greece in the West and China in the East; in its subsequent evolution and growth of insight, it achieves a stature which corresponds with the Golden Ages of Christian and Muslim theological attainment.

From the years when the Aryan peoples pushed down into the northern plains and river areas of India, there to meet the indigenous Dravidian culture which was not without its own potential contributions, the Indian people have been embarked upon a philosophical-theological path which has elevated them among the peoples of the world. From this concern there has flowed a stream of thought which has bequeathed its legacy not only upon the Indian people, but upon much of the eastern world. Basic presuppositions were established which have become not only the foundation of subsequent Indian thought but also of much of the philosophical and religious systems of eastern Asia. A world view was created that may be said to be the primary element that gives eastern philosophy and religion their historic and present nature.

Today, after some three thousand years of development, Hindu philosophy continues to play a dominant role in the area of its beginnings and growth. The spirit of the old Hindustan and the thought of the new India are not only related but in large measure identical because of the persistence of the Hindu *Weltanschauung* which this philosophy produced and has continued to make relevant. The encroachment of western thought and civilization in all of its aspects has had its effect upon Hindu philosophy, as well as upon Indian life and society; but it has not appreciably dimmed the vigor of the thought and fundamental concepts which are to be identified with the essence of traditional Hindu philosophy. On the contrary, under this impact Hindu thought today is expressing itself in a forceful and energetic manner.

In adjacent nations, cultures, and religions this same legacy has its exponents who are asserting its value for the world today through derivative systems which trace much of their basic thought to India. The primary instance of this is Buddhism which, in its many varied forms, is a native expression of what was Indian in origin. Though historic development may have taken it far afield from its peculiar Indian beginnings, the fundamental and still essential pillars which support its present assertions are unmistakably derived from, and related to, the thought-world of its birth. As a result, the traditional values of Indian philosophy are laying claim to contemporary and universal relevance through religions and philosophies which have already been enriched by contact with, and expression in, cultural areas non-Indian in their origin.

All who have more than a cursory acquaintance with Indian religion and philosophy are aware of the problem which arises in the attempt to define just what is meant by the term Hinduism. Is Hinduism specifically a religion, a group of philosophical systems, a social structure with its attendant customs and mores, or something which is more broadly and more correctly designated as a culture? Is it any one of these, or a combination of some or all of them? An adequate and defensible answer to this question would take us into a long and detailed study of the involved history of India, as well as requiring us to digress into the problems which arise in any endeavor to isolate one part of a total cultural entity from its necessary partners in the aggregate and from their collective development.

The problem is further complicated, in an investigation such as ours, by the absence of what may properly be termed theology within the Hindu context. In all areas of intellectual endeavor, philosophy and theology have had their periods of identity and similarity. Since, as we have previously indicated, they are often, if not always, concerned with the same ultimate questions, it is to be expected that they will intersect and overlap. In India's intellectual history what might be termed theology in the West, has been subsumed under philosophy in much the same manner that philosophy was but a part of theology in periods of western Christian history. As a result, we shall speak of Indian and Hindu philosophy, rather than of Hindu theology.[1]

Our problem in defining Hinduism is also complicated by the traditional and prevailing western custom of using the term primarily with a religious connotation. Of course, this is done in the case of the names which are given to each of the religions we are discussing, and the problem as to the separation of a religion from the whole body of its historic associations and products is an enormous one.

In the case of Hinduism, there is a body of ancient and subsequent thought and insight which has created the totality of Indian philosophy, religion, society, culture, and all else which is to be identified as being primarily Indian. Each and all of these may or may not, in all observable instances, attain the level of the highest ideals which are properly associated with the best of the early and succeeding systems of thought. No one of them is *Hinduism* in its fullest sense. All, separately and collectively, must be recognized to be parts, and undoubtedly essential ones, of the historic unfolding of the Hindu religious experience as it has matured and affected Indian and eastern civilization.

For our purposes, we shall attempt to gain insight and understanding of Hinduism through a consideration of the philosophy which has created the foundations upon which the totality of Hinduism is erected. This means that the cultic and social expressions of Hinduism, which are essential and predominant aspects of any religion, will not be our primary concern. It does not mean, however, that our study can assume that they are unnecessary appendages which have no intrinsic value for the philosophy historically associated with them. No religion in the past has been able to exist only as a theology or philosophy, and it is doubtful that any will succeed in doing so.

It is in and through the contributions of Hindu philosophy that Hinduism will have its primary place in the future of religious thought. It is Hindu philosophy which will most effectively and precisely serve as a partner with Buddhist philosophy, Christian theology, and Muslim theology in the development of a system or systems or religious thought which will have significance for the immediate and distant future of mankind. It is only when Hindu philosophy ventures forth into full conversation with these other traditional, and still dynamic philosophical-theological systems, that its own inherited values will achieve the universal consideration it considers to be their due. Hindu thought may make part of its impact upon the world through its manifestations within its own traditional social and cultural boundaries, but the significant contributions potential within it demand that it venture out further from the parochial restrictions which it has known in the past.

1

India has not been conscious of history in the manner and degree that has been typical of the West. It would appear that pre-modern Indian writers even sought to ignore history. However, while it is obvious that a fundamental characteristic of Indian thought, from its beginnings, has been an indifference to history, this indifference has been a natural result of the Hindu attitude toward Time more than it has been the product of a deliberate attempt to obscure the historic processes and events which have occurred within the Indian area. The Hindu has traditionally understood Time to be cyclical in nature, not linear. Thought, and even events, do not gain their importance because of their place in the movement of Time; the significance of an item of belief or a change in political or social structure is not to be reckoned on the basis of the specific time of its appearance. Truth or value are to be understood ultimately apart from the relative and insignificant matter of when they were revealed or discovered. The fundamental problem in areas of human knowledge and in affairs of human activity is related to a question of much greater depth than one of sequence in time. An adequate understanding of the Hindu view of History, or Time, would be dependent upon a separate study beyond our primary concern. It would reveal, I believe, not so much that Hinduism has no doctrine of History as is often charged by western scholars, as that Hinduism

has an understanding or doctrine of Time so different from any held
in the West that the categories which are familiar and meaningful
to the West are not applicable.[2]

The foregoing is pertinent to our present discussion because it
serves to remind us that a study of the development of Hindu
thought is forced to be somewhat different from the study of the
evolution of western thought. While we do face the difficulty of not
always being able to ascribe a particular writing, or founding of a
school of thought, to a specific thinker, especially in the early periods of western philosophy or religion, in the case of India even an
approximation is impossible in some instances. It is only rarely that
a specific body of writing or collection of thought can be ascribed to
a particular person, and even then the lack of historically founded
knowledge about the person leaves him in the haze of legend rather
than being grounded in established historic fact. However, in the
Hindu view it is the content of the thought and its significance for
human understanding that is of particular importance, not the time,
nor the historic person who said it.

Nevertheless, it is essential to our understanding of Hindu philosophy that we be aware of the successive periods of its formation and
development. Obviously, philosophy does not spring into existence
full grown, nor is its growth a simple uninvolved process without
digression and retrogression. The various modern histories of Indian
Philosophy give detailed accounts of the separate periods of Indian
thought and their divers schools.[3] Our hope to gain appreciation of
the potential contributions of Hindu philosophy to the modern
world requires that we be cognizant of at least the major factors and
currents in the history of Indian thought.

While scholars have not been able to establish precisely the time
of the Aryan migration into India, it is agreed that sometime before
1000 B.C. the Aryans had succeeded in gaining a predominant place
for themselves in the region of the river valleys of the north, with
the result that they were free to establish their own culture with
minor interference from outside. This is not to suggest that local
and pre-Aryan culture did not exert influence upon what might be
considered to be primarily Aryan. Recent scholarship has continued
to reveal that a higher level of indigenous civilization existed than
had previously been believed. We are also able to discover pre-Aryan

deposits which continued to exist and express themselves within the totality of Aryan culture. However, the society which was established by about 1000 B.C. in northern India, and which has continued down to today as the predominant cultural ethos of India, was primarily the product of the Aryan peoples, and continues to be their legacy.[4]

The hymns of the Rig Veda reflect a noble and heroic people pushing on into a new and strange land. They reveal the thoughts of poets, not the reflections of philosophers. Like the Psalmists of the Hebrews they were seeking after God; they were beseeching evidences of protection and affinity, searching for that for which their hearts longed and their intellects only dimly perceived.

The hymns disclose a worship of semi-personified forces of nature and an almost hidden substructure of earlier and simultaneous primitive religious beliefs and practices. The religion of the poet is not the religion of the philosopher; nor is it the religion of the average man who lacks the intuitive insight and longing which sets the poet apart from his fellows, causing him to speak of things more sublime than the ordinary. We can be quite certain that, as the thought of the Psalmists rose above the religious level of their fellow Hebrews, so too, the reflections of the creators of the Vedic hymns ascend beyond the religious limitations of the majority of their fellow men.

While this distinction is important in that it prevents us from mistakenly assuming a highly advanced religion, far removed from the generally primitive level of the religion of the time, a factor of prime importance in the development of Indian religion would be overlooked if we were to emphasize the distinction without noting the relationship. This relationship reminds us that the creations of the religious poet are dependent upon the religious environment and foundation out of which he comes. He may, and probably does, make a leap beyond his religious tradition. But he takes that leap from the platform of his inherited environment.

There was within the religious experience of the Aryan peoples an element of insight which led to a searching which would not be satisfied with the simple or the traditional. Those of the early Aryans who were of a religious and poetic nature were following the inner impulse of the collective religious experience of their people.

And to a rather startling degree, the religious expressions of the Indian people have continued to reflect much of the spirit which is to be found in the Vedic hymns.

It is in these hymns that we discern the first attempts to get behind both the lesser and the greater gods to the unity which it was felt must be their source. The religious seers of the Vedas were conscious of the tremendous quality of the forces of nature, and discerned in them an element which was superior to the god or gods with which they were associated. They were stepping beyond the restrictions resulting from the personification of primary forces of existence into a realm where any degree of anthropomorphism was recognized as being not only inadequate, but misleading. Like the dramatists and philosophers of early Greece, they were seeking a higher unity of which the separate forces seen by man were but manifestations.

And most startling of all, there is the occasional attempt by these religious geniuses to ascertain, in all the variety and complexity of human and supra-human existence, a unity and an inherent relationship which encompasses both gods and men, a unity of both material existence and the ultimate law or essence which is its foundation.[5] And while the full statement and culmination of such thinking was to come at a later time, by this poetic expression the religiously inspired seers of early India blazed the trail which was to become the distinctive path of Hindu thought in the majority of its expressions from then on to the present.

It was in the hymns of the Rig Veda that the foundation was laid for subsequent Hindu thought, as, in the Rig and other Vedas, the basic substructure and wellsprings of the religion of later Hinduism were grounded. The common acknowledgment of the authority of the Vedas has been the most general unifying element in Hinduism. The rules for ritual, the authority for guidance in the religious life, are first to be found here. As subsequent philosophical-theological writings were to make their claim to authority on the ground that they were but enlargements and interpretations of the truths adumbrated in the Vedas, so too were the priestly and cultic elements of all later Hinduism to exact their prerogatives on the basis of this authority. Even the later lower levels of the religion of the countryside, which had their origins in local indigenous cults, achieved their "Hindu" status by relating themselves in one fashion or another to the Vedic authority.

The Vedic hymns, therefore, serve as the fountainhead of Indian religion and Hindu philosophy. In the midst of the almost Olympian nature of their deities there is revealed a probing and searching which reflects an inquisitiveness of mind and a sensitivity of spirit that was to become the pattern of subsequent Hindu thought. From that time on the philosophical-religious thinkers of India searched further for the Unity which lies behind the diversity of human experience and the Order *(rita)* which gives uniformity and symmetry to all existence. The direction in which their probing must proceed was laid down in the early Aryan hymns that continue to be their orientation today.[6]

Simultaneously with the hymns of the Rig Veda, and in the period immediately following them, Indian religion also exhibited a major concern for the observance of sacrifice properly performed. This is revealed to us most clearly in the Brahmanas, the treatises on ritual which reveal the mind of the priest rather than that of the poet. The result was a sacrificial religion in which the priest became supreme, and the worshiper was required to engage in a mechanical and uninspiring ritual which seldom lifted him beyond the mundane. Sacrificial ritual does give the religious person a consciousness of the universe beyond himself and his society; it seldom leads him to the contemplation, meditation, and introspection which results in productive religious sensitivity, or philosophical-theological insights. From the perspective of Hindu philosophy and thought, the Brahmanas reveal a period of decadence which did not measure up to the potentialities dimly, yet dynamically, foreshadowed in the hymns of the Rig Veda.

It was in the Upanishads that the promise of the poets of the Rig Veda was brought to fruition. As is the case in the history of most bodies of literature and their related cultural developments, it would not be accurate to separate the hymns of the Rig Veda, the Brahmanas, and the Upanishads from one another in a definite chronological sequence, as if when one was produced in final form, the other then followed. While it is erroneous to imply that all were produced simultaneously, it is essential that we understand that the latter two flourished side by side. Both are to be classed as Vedic

literature in that they supplement the early Vedas and find their
authority in them; but, while the Brahmanas are the supporters of
the cultic aspects of religion, the Upanishads are the disturbers of
that which is the accepted and traditional in the religion of the
time.

Written as *Vedanta*, the end and aim of the Vedas, the Upanishads serve as the real source for the later currents of Hindu
thought. Philosophical treatises of the highest order, they set the
form and structure which Hindu philosophy was to follow from the
time of their origin on to the present. They reveal a combination of
the spirit of the poet and the brilliance of the philosopher. They
reflect the sensitivity of the man of religion as he unites that sensitivity with the resources of his intellect. Surprisingly uninhibited in
the range of their reflection and probing they, nevertheless, demonstrate a unity within themselves as they deliberate upon the nature
of the truth which is behind, within, and beyond existence.

Our later consideration of the central themes of Hindu philosophy will be in large measure a discussion of the basic presuppositions which recur throughout the Upanishads. The fundamental
categories and conceptions of Indian thought today continue to be
those which first received their definitive formulation in the philosophical-theological discussions which constitute the Upanishads.
Brahman, Ātman, Samsāra, Karma, Dharma, Moksha, Maya—these,
and other themes which compose the heart of Hindu philosophy,
are brought into clear focus as the upanishadic thinkers delve into
the mysteries which confront all reflective men.

The venture of the Hindu spirit, to which the Upanishads call
the thinkers of India, is one wherein the mind is engaged but is not
supreme, the emotions are involved but are not dominant, words are
used but are not adequate, gods are conceived but are not sufficient,
and man is challenged to religious pilgrimage but is not alone in his
striving. In short, a philosophy which demanded severe application
of the powers of the human intellect, combined with the most pro-
found sensitivity of the religious resources of man to become the
greatest treasure of India.[7]

At the time of the appearance of Buddhism and Jainism in the
sixth century B.C., religion in India consisted of low levels of cultic
practice and belief among the masses of the people, alongside a high

attainment of philosophical-theological conversation and insight limited to a very few. The faint, but persistent, gains of the hymns of the Rig Veda, which had been brought into bold relief by the Upanishads, were all but submerged under the religious practices of the people and the priests. Indian religion was conservative and stultifying; it was not adventuresome, nor was it demanding upon the religiously sensitive.

Both Buddhism and Jainism in their earliest stages may properly be understood as reforming groups within Hinduism. To a large degree they continued the highest ideals to be found in the Hindu past, and they expressed their thought in terms and by means which were in keeping with the Indian religious tradition. In the case of Buddhism especially, many of the fundamental presuppositions which were at the base of the upanishadic philosophic speculations were central to the new teaching. And even those few which were rejected, exerted a covert influence upon the developing Buddhist thought. While the two new movements did not accept the authority of the Vedas, and spoke out in strong protest against the power of the priests and the cultic centrality of the vedic sacrifices they, nevertheless, originally understood themselves to be advances within the Hindu tradition and not total seceders from it. Though small in numbers, Jainism has succeeded in maintaining itself as a contributing element within Indian life through the centuries,[8] and Buddhism, for a significant period of history, was a leading religion of India.

While we shall discuss Buddhism in more detail in a later chapter, it is interesting and important to note that some Hindu scholars of today treat Buddhism as a significant contribution to Hindu thought.[9] Their philosophical-theological tolerance allows Hindu scholars to recognize that the ideals of early Buddhism were more in line with the insights of the composers of the Upanishads than was the priestly religion of the time. The fact that in certain basic presuppositions of upanishadic and subsequent Hindu philosophy, Gotama and his successors radically departed from the developing Hindu tradition is seen as a tribute to the breadth and inherent truth of Hinduism, rather than as a denial of it. The strength of early Buddhist thought and practice, and its affinity to Indian religious longings, is demonstrated by its centuries of existence as a dominant religion in large areas of India. The persistence of the popular Hinduism of the people, and the Hindu philosophy of the scholars, is evidenced by the eventual triumph in India of Hinduism over Buddhism.

The recovery of Hinduism from the inroads of Buddhism was brought about, in large measure, by the contributions of the great epics and other popular literature at about the beginning of the Christian era. While probably earlier in origin, the Ramayana, the Mahabharata, and other specifically Hindu oral and literary products received in the four or five centuries from about 200 B.C. the form which, by and large, they have carried down to the present. There was thus a Hindu renaissance in which the more specifically Hindu religion of India turned from retreat to advance in the face of Buddhism.

In this rebirth of Hindu religious strength the two great epics, the Ramayana and the Mahabharata, combined with the development of other popular literature (*Puranas*) to convey to the Indian people in myth, legend, and story the central religious concepts which were enshrined in the more philosophic and scholarly literature generally known only to the priests and scholars. The stories of great heroes were made to convey, through event and dialogue, the teachings which were the Aryan contribution to Indian thought. Hinduism's revival was the direct result of the combination of sophisticated philosophical-theological thought with the popular religious beliefs and customs of the common man. While the gulf between these two levels was not, of course, eradicated, a more advanced and common core of beliefs among great numbers of the Indian people was established to an extent which had not previously existed.

It may be said that the appearance of Jainism and Buddhism, the latter in particular, served as a catalyst to give content and greater unity to the variety and vast difference in levels of the Hinduism of the time. The variety, which has continued to be so typical of Hindu religion, did not disappear, but a minimal common body of philosophical assumptions or presuppositions were more firmly established as the unifying foundation throughout Hinduism's diversity. It is this heritage of the Upanishads which makes it possible for us to speak of a Hindu religion when we refer to the wide variety in Indian religion. Now embodied in a popular oral and literary tradition, their insights enabled the earlier religious poets and philosophical thinkers to increase their influence upon the whole of the developing Indian culture.

In this process the more specifically religious elements of Indian society, and the culture as a whole, were brought under the influence of both the religious insights of the thinkers and the religious yearnings of the common people. In the Epic Age, Hinduism forged a strong link between these two levels of its religious heritage by bringing reflective and philosophical thought into the ethos of the popular religion, and it also lifted religious elements, which were at the heart of the religion of the devout worshiper, into the more philosophical realm.

A theism was given a place to flourish within the more impersonal and abstract atmosphere of the Hindu philosophy which, heretofore, had been distinct from popular beliefs. The somewhat cold and involved thought of the scholars was now receptive to the warmth and personal constituents of popular religion. And while Hindu philosophy in many of its expressions has not always accepted personal theism as being allowable at the level of ultimate religious and philosophical truth, it has generally given it a respected place. Religiously, if not always philosophically, speaking, the epic literature established as an intrinsic part of Hindu orthodoxy a personal God (*Ishvara*) who is identified with the creation and ordering of existence. In like manner to the understanding of the deities of popular religion, this personal God is responsive to the devotion and supplication of the worshiper.

In conjunction with this more meaningful union of philosophy and religion within the Hindu ethos, various religious doctrines were firmly established within the Indian religious mind and tradition. The doctrine of God in a threefold aspect of creation, preservation, and destruction (*Trimurti*) and the doctrine of the incarnation of God in human form (*Avatara*) are of primary importance for the future of Hinduism. The Divine is not totally removed; It is involved in the ordering of existence and society to the degree that the problems of men move the Divine to appear in their midst to teach them and receive their devotion. The Divine possesses compassion which leads to involvement with man's mundane problems, and it is this divine concern which is the source of man's hope and the means for his final fulfilment in this life and beyond.

We thus have, by the early centuries of the Christian era, the establishment of Indian philosophy and Hindu religion in the basic mold which has typified it ever since. The philosophical and impersonal Absolute (*Brahman*) and the personal deity (*Ishvara*) are available to the worshiper. The fundamental philosophical-theological presuppositions such as rebirth, Karma, Avatara, and the other elements which we shall presently consider serve as the substructure upon which the Hindu mind-set is based and are the recurring themes of Hinduism. Above all, the union and tension between philosophy and religion occurred, which gave Hinduism the necessary strength to be a dynamic and viable primary force in the life of the Indian people.

In the centuries following the Epic Age and the union between religion and philosophy, the sectarian Puranas reflect a growing religious vitality which was accompanied by a sectarian rivalry resulting from the rise of groups devoting themselves to one deity in an exclusive manner. The relatively mild sectarian theism of the epics was succeeded by movements leading toward an exclusive monotheism in which the tolerance inherent to Hinduism was severely strained. The worshipers of Vishnu, Shiva, and Sakti each came to see, in his own devotion and cult, the one best way for the attainment of divine protection and favor.

Within each group the worshiper came to find in the specific god and his divine associates all that was needed for religious satisfaction and support. In each instance, Puranic literature and tradition developed to give support to the religious beliefs and practices of the group. And in the structure and further development of such groups, they began to relate their deities and their religious beliefs to hospitable elements present in the emerging philosophical schools of Hindu thought.

By about the seventh and eighth centuries A.D., Hinduism was thus in a state of rapid resurgence against a Buddhism which, in India, had lost its appeal and momentum. In the struggle with Buddhism, Hinduism had united its divergent forces and brought into being the fundamental ethos of thought and codes of belief and practice which have continued to be essential to it. It had laid the foundation for the development of separate philosophical schools within the framework of its traditional philosophic structure, and had created an atmosphere well suited for the rise of the greatest thinkers in its history in the immediately succeeding centuries. The first among these great philosopher-theologians, Shankara, was probably born in the latter decades of the eighth century.[10] Very little is known about his life except that, though short, it was one of great intellectual achievement combined with practical activity. Shankara was the champion of what was to become, in general, the orthodox interpretation of the Vedas and Upanishads in contra-distinction to Buddhism, as well as to Hindu schools of philosophy and religious thought which, to his mind, were departing from the true Vedanta. There has been a strong tendency in the western world to identify the teachings of Shankara with Hinduism as if all Hindu thinkers were strict adherents to his thought. It must be recognized that he is not the only Hindu philosopher and that, par-ticularly in matters of religious metaphysics, others have had equal or greater impact upon Hindu belief. However, in a manner some-what analogous to the function and place of Augustine and Aquinas in the development of Christian thought and theological orthodoxy, Shankara did construct the interpretation of the essence of the Vedas and Upanishads which was to be predominant in acceptance and influence. All subsequent Hindu philosophy was indebted to it, either directly or indirectly, for even when there were departures from it, there was awareness of the need to try to refute its power-ful claims.

Our later consideration of the basic themes of Hindu philosophy will be directly concerned with the predominant features of Shan-kara's system. However, it is necessary at this point to make brief mention of the following: first, Shankara maintained that there is only one ultimate Reality—That toward which the seers of old were pointing in the hymns of the Rig Veda and That which the philosophers of the Upanishads termed Brahman; second, the ultimate Reality is not to be known by man through conceptual knowledge nor any form of belief, practice, or attitude, but only by the illumination (*jñāna*) which results from a type of meditation that produces the realization that the ultimate Reality and the self (*ātman*) of man are identical; and, third, release (*moksha*) from the world of rebirth and the continuous wheel of existence (*samsāra*) is therefore dependent upon the overcoming of the ignorance (*avidyā*) which leads man to think of himself as a separate self whose essential being is dependent upon causality (*karma*). The intricacy and depth of this sophisticated and rich system of thought cannot, of course, be even faintly suggested in the foregoing few sentences. The philosophy of Shankara is an absolute non-dualism (*Advaita*) wherein the famous phrase in the Upanishads, "That art Thou," (*tat tvam asi*) is the declaration that Brahman (Ultimate Reality) equals Ātman (the self) and Ātman equals Brahman.

Also of great importance in the development of Hindu philosophy-theology, perhaps more so in relation to the religious life of Hinduism, was Ramanuja, the second outstanding Hindu thinker, the great Bhakti saint of the twelfth century. Inheriting the strong south Indian religious tradition of adoration and devotion (*bhakti*) to the Divine, Ramanuja gave to Bhakti the philosophical setting needed to ground it in the Vedic and upanishadic metaphysics. While Shankara's religion was primarily a mysticism stated in philosophic language, Ramanuja's philosophy was first and foremost an expression of warmhearted religion seeking to justify itself within the philosophic tradition of India.[11]

Ramanuja's contribution, therefore, was the unification of philosophy and popular religion, the bringing together, in an acceptable fashion, of the traditional philosophy of the Upanishads with the religious spirit to be identified, in particular, with the bhakti movement among the people of south India. He united the philosophical Absolute with the theistic Deity, or at least succeeded in removing the gulf and inherent antipathy between them in order that both could exist within the greater whole of the Hindu ethos. Unlike Shankara who recognized only one ultimate Reality, Ramanuja conceived of three ultimate Realities, namely, God, soul, and matter. However, soul and matter must be understood to be in a relationship of absolute dependence upon God. Taken together the three are a unity, and the latter two are inseparable from the first. The whole of Ramanuja's system is a qualified non-dualism (*Visistadvaita*) or qualified monism, in which all is derived from, and dependent upon, the Absolute or Divine, yet, once in existence, possesses a limited separateness. For Ramanuja, instead of the *absolute* identity between the ultimate Reality and the true human self maintained by Shankara, the Divine which has produced existence is in intrinsic relationship with the self, or soul, of man.

On the basis of the foregoing, salvation or release (*moksha*) is not to be received or gained by a realization of the absolute identity of the Brahman and Ātman, but is the fruit of adoration (*bhakti*) and total self-surrender (*prapatti*) to the God of grace (*Bhagavat*). And, of primary importance to the appeal and popularity of the many Bhakti sects which were to be the leading influence in so much of subsequent Hinduism, self-surrender to God, says Ramanuja, is not limited by caste status or formal religious preparation. It is a path of salvation available to all.

At the same time that the popular religion, exemplified by Bhakti, was obtaining a status of orthodoxy within the Hindu philosophical-theological system under the leadership of scholars such as Ramanuja, a literary tradition, both oral and written, was increasing and supporting the spread of a commonly held body of religious beliefs. The first beginnings of translations of the great epics into the vernacular languages, and the appearance of works such as the Bhagavata Purana, set the stage for much of the popular religious belief and lore which remains even today central to Hinduism. Through the medium of the Bhagavata Purana the childhood and life of the god Krishna furnished, to great numbers of the Indian people, a basis for song and drama which nourished their religious life and brought joy to their daily activities.

In the realm of philosophical-theological thought, the succeeding centuries were marked by the continued existence of the basic philosophical speculation and categories which first appeared most clearly in the Upanishads. The so-called "Six Schools of Indian Philosophy," divergent among themselves and giving widely different interpretations to aspects of upanishadic thought were, however, generally accepted as being within the orthodox tradition. The breadth of the Hindu propensity for tolerance and acceptance of variety in matters of philosophy and religion is illustrated by the inclusiveness of the conception of orthodoxy. Also, systems of thought continued to appear and, in instances such as that of the unqualified dualism (*Dvaita*) of Madhva, exerted strong influence upon religious thought and practice. To a large extent, religious interests predominated over what the westerner would classify as more specifically philosophical; but once Hindu religious thought has risen above the most primary of levels, the two, of course, are not to be separated.

Thus it was that from the time Muslim power was established over the greater portion of India, from the thirteenth down to the nineteenth century, the most important religious developments have had an influence upon the philosophical situation of today and will influence the theological thought of the future. The fundamental philosophical outlook, which we have associated with the Upanishads, underwent little, if any, change. Indian thought was confined to commentary and constructions upon that foundation. It was, however, in the frequent rise of religious leaders and saints that Hinduism continued to establish itself as the base of Indian life and culture. It was in the continued appearance of new religious movements, usually of the Bhakti type, that Hinduism was able to restore and maintain its energy as a viable religious faith for the Indian people.

A mere listing of the religious geniuses of these centuries, and a brief account of their teachings and movements would require considerable space.[12] Despite their separate importance and contributions to Indian religion, their full and collective gift, to the Hinduism of their time and of the present, was the development and continued nourishment of a religion of sensitive and deep devotion to the particular aspect or incarnation of the Divine which they worshiped. From the intense emotional love of Ramananda for Rama, the incarnation of Vishnu, to the poetic and fervent adoration of Tulsi Das, or the devotion of Tukaram to Krishna, or the self-surrender of those who worshiped the Divine Mother, the whole gamut of Hindu religious life was caught up in an urgent and unceasing search for relationship with the Divine. The breadth and sensitivity to religious insight of the Indian people, whatever the source, were evidenced by Kabir and by Nanak; their allegiance to their specifically Hindu past was demonstrated by the language, art, and ritual of their religious thought and life.

In each case the Hindu groups, which were a part of this great Bhakti movement, preached a salvation through adoration and devotion to the one supreme deity, whatever His or Her name or manifestation. Devotion and self-surrender were the keynotes. The sincere love of a man for the God whose primary characteristic or quality is grace, is of even greater value than the intellectual speculation, meditation, and mystic path of the scholarly religious recluse grounded in the ancient knowledge of the Vedas and Upanishads though, of course, this was not acknowledged by such scholars. The Bhakti movements and their adherents lifted much of popular Hinduism above the mechanical ritual and primitivism of the past, while it brought some of the religious insights of the philosophers down into the fabric of the religion of the people.

This, in brief, was the situation within the Hindu philosophic and religious ethos at the beginning of the nineteenth century. We have not been able to chart the course of development in detail, nor have we given attention to the wide diversity of levels in sophistication, morality, religious sensitivity, and fervor which varied from area to area and from group to group. It should be sufficient to say that Hinduism, like all great religions, had its weaknesses and its strengths as a part of Indian life, its periods of lethargy and of vitality, its leaders who were merely holders of position and those who were dynamic—in short, it was a religion, a world-view, and a way of life both guiding and sharing the moods and fortunes of its people.

2

The basic and recurring themes of Hindu philosophy have been briefly suggested in our discussion of the development of Indian religion and thought from Vedic times up to the beginning of the modern period, about the opening of the nineteenth century. As we have emphasized, these fundamental presuppositions of the Indian thought-world were, in part, foreshadowed in the Vedic writings, and, by the time of the composition of the leading Upanishads, were firmly entrenched in the fertile philosophic atmosphere of India. From that time on they have served to structure and direct Indian thought. No system of Indian philosophy or religion has been able to escape coming to grips with these themes. In the majority of instances such propositions have been positive and leading elements in the systems; in some cases they have been disavowed, but even such rejection has served to give a particular nature to the system which it would have lacked had the negation not been made.

We have noted that very early, Indian thought was concerned with the question of order in the structure of existence. In their perception of the environment and their sensitivity to that which lay behind it, the early thinkers discerned a uniformity and pattern despite the sometimes chaotic external appearance of existence and events. There is a power, a law or unity of laws which constitutes the Order (*rita*) of empirical existence. Like the Tao of Chinese thought, it is that Power which works in and through the universe of being, directing the individual powers and entities toward symmetry and meaning in their collective activities. And, while its working or movement may possibly be discernible to man, its purposes, or lack of them, are beyond man's ultimate understanding.

In conjunction with the emergence of such thinking, there was the growing conviction that, behind all that is, is a Unity which includes within Itself that which appears, from the perspective of man, to be disparate and non-cohesive. In the early periods of beginning speculation this was limited mainly to a unification of the separate deities and their powers, but even at this early stage the unification was more in the nature of an identification wherein the individual deities were coming to be conceived not so much as distinct entities gathered together into a greater whole, but rather as one undivided Unity perceived by man in different aspects or functions.

With the coalescence of this conception of Order (*rita*) with the conviction of a Unity (*Brahman*), there was a resultant flowering of the belief in a divine order and propriety of things, a Dharma which extends to all existence and beings. And while the word Dharma has many meanings and usages, each of them conveys, at least in part, the thought of a transcendental, yet imminent and all encompassing imperative norm inherent in the structure of existence. The empirical realm has its Dharma, all sentient life has its Dharma, and man in particular has his Dharma as an individual and as a member of society. This Dharma flows from the absolute Unity which is at the beginning, middle, and end of all things. It is a norm which is integrally inherent in its Source (*Brahman*) and is not to be conceived as separate from It. It is of the nature of the Unity behind the apparent diversity of existence that It, in Itself, gives to the universe of being a structure, a pattern, a *telos*.

We must be careful to note here that such Order is not to be considered as necessarily meaningful or conformable to human standards. Human perceptions of order are derivable from this inherent structure, but the structure is not to be appraised by anything other than itself. The value of the Order, therefore, its goodness or its evil, is not a legitimate matter for speculation or question. The Order is what It is, and because of It, there is that which is proper and improper, valuable and non-valuable. The given is good, in a metaphysical sense, simply because it is given. There is nothing else that is possible since all potentiality is embodied in the given.

Students of philosophy and theology will realize that the foregoing is but an elementary and preliminary statement of a type of reasoning which, by its nature, is fertile ground for a variety of speculation and conclusions. One example should suffice to indicate the danger of overlooking the ramifications in a brief presentation of thought which possesses such potential complexities. Given these two presuppositions of Order and Unity, how is it possible to bestow upon a thing or an event the qualities of value or disvalue? Would it not appear that all that has been, now is, or potentially may be, exists because of the Order which is of the inherent nature of the Unity? Is there any thing or event conceivable which could be thought to have arisen ultimately outside of, or apart from the Unity? And, if all that has its being is, therefore, traceable back to, or to a part of, the Unity and its inherent Order, would it not follow that to ascribe non-value to anything would be to predicate a characteristic of non-value to the ultimate Unity Itself? Since the Absolute Unity is *sui generis,* and the ultimate source and norm of all being and all value, is it at all possible for a derivative of that Unity, man, to possess any norm greater than the norm which is integral to the Unity? The obvious result is, of course, that one must be driven to the conclusion that standards and judgments such as value or disvalue are not absolute or defensible in an ultimate sense. At most they are always relative and of pertinence only in the mundane choices of men. And, even here the thinker will be aware that such decisions are of no ultimate consequence.

Such inevitable conclusions from basic metaphysical presuppositions were to have great importance in the development of Hindu philosophy. The example we have given was to create for Hindu ethics a position which western thinkers, particularly theologians, have generally found to be difficult to understand or to use as a base for human action. It was at this point that the famous Bhagavad-Gita made its great contribution to Hindu ethical thought and life.[13] Given the ultimate Unity (*Brahman*) and the inherent Order of existence, which means, as we have suggested, that the given is not of any intrinsic value or disvalue as such, each man has the particular Order (*Dharma*) which he must follow because of his own peculiar situation or station in existence. It is not for the individual to concern himself with anything other than the duty (*dharma*) which is incumbent upon him. In the ultimate metaphysical sense his duty is the resultant of *the* Order of all existence or being, it is an imperative imposed upon him by the structure of things. However, even here this duty is to be understood in most schools of Hindu philosophy as being limited, as far as real consequence is involved, to the realm of empirical existence. It is not of *ultimate* universal import.

Given the assumption of an ultimate Order or structure of being (and non-being) and the predication of an ultimate Unity, it follows that ground is laid for certain conceptions of the nature of the Unity and of its derivatives such as the world of existence and man. It was at this point that the thinkers who produced the Upanishads revealed both the subtlety of their philosophical-theological insight, and the strict and demanding nature of their logic. They were deeply conscious of the immensity of the realm of existence and they were sensitive to the limitations of human thought and its perceptions.

When they considered Brahman they realized, first of all, that human categories were insufficient to deal with That which was, by nature, beyond them. Brahman is not limited to the realm of empirical existence and, therefore, must be unlimited in Its nature. Yet, since It is the source of all being It cannot be said to be *abso-*

lutely different from being. Existing beyond being as well as within it, it would follow that Brahman is related to or includes non-being also. However, is it possible to speak of Brahman as existing? Existence is a category of human thought which rests upon the human perception of empirical objects, events, or thoughts. It is a statement of being as against non-being, and Brahman, as ultimate Unity, is not simply the unity of existing being. If Brahman or Unity does not include all potential being which as yet is non-being, It would not be ultimate Unity but only a unity limited to the presently created. There would need to be Something greater, and it would be this Greater which would be *the* Unity, not Brahman.

All forms of human speech, categories of human thought, and potential horizons of human speculation are, obviously, insufficient to take man conceptually to the level of Brahman. For at any level reached, there remains That which is dimly perceived intellectually as being higher or greater, and This is Brahman. Yet, Brahman is not the next step which man cannot conceptualize; Brahman is the ultimate level toward which the human mind cannot in reality positively progress at all. The intellectual endeavors of man can at the most, perhaps, chart out the broad outlines of the structure of the existence derivative from Brahman and not ultimate in itself, but even this is more negative than positive in nature.

Since the time of the philosophers of the Upanishads, Hindu philosophy has had as a basic theme the ultimate unknowable nature of the Brahman. Like many great philosophies in the world's history, it has intimated something of the nature of the Absolute by its procedure of negating all positive empirical predicates which might be applied to It. Unlike most theologies, it has refused to ascribe characteristics or ideal qualities since, from the perspective of philosophy, they inevitably involve an element of human judgment or ideal hopes.

The latter matter was, as we have seen, the function of Hindu theism within the Indian ethos. Any distinction made in Hindu intellectual speculation between philosophy and theology could possibly be made at this point. That is to say, Hindu religious thought which is non-theistic is not theology as the term is usually understood in the West. Hindu religious thought which is theistic does participate in matters which are more akin to the theological

concerns of the western world. However, where western theology,
though influenced by philosophy in many ways, considers itself
finally to be determined by the limits of the revelation upon which
it is founded, the form and structure of Hindu theistic thought is
determined by the philosophical tradition of India. True, the Vedas
are revelation (*sruti*) and, also, the theistic groups are centered
about the revelations of incarnations (*avataras*) of the Divine Absolute, but there is an element of authority in the basic metaphysical
presuppositions of India which has not existed generally in the case
of western theologies. It is this fact which has given Hinduism much
of its unique quality when it is seen in comparison with the religions
associated with the western world. In both areas, of course, there
has been an overt and covert marriage between what is to be
termed specifically philosophy and specifically theology. Both have
created the thought-world of their areas. However, especially in the
formative period of intellectual growth and solidification, the
authority of the non-theistic and philosophic thought of the scholars in India was primary, and theistic theology was required to
adjust itself to it. And, while both Christianity and Islam have
been greatly dependent upon philosophy for many of their categories of thought and their highest intellectual expressions, they
have had at their base a body of revelation which they have considered in no way to be subject, in a final sense, to the norms of
philosophic thought.

The distinction here is a fine one which is difficult to comprehend
fully without long and sustained acquaintance with the religious
thought of the East and the West. India, too, in its understanding
of the source of any human comprehension of truth, has a central
place for divine revelation. However, for Hindu thought, the nature
and extent of revelation is not identical in scope or finality with
that of the western or Semitic religions and their theologies, nor in
the West is philosophy identified with the divine revelation to
nearly the degree that it is in Hinduism. Philosophy may have a
place in the natural revelation which is sometimes acknowledged
by western theologians, it may even be of direct aid in the support
of theology, but it comes from a source which is not of the stature
or ultimacy of divine revelation.

As a result, the theistic schools of thought within Hinduism

sought to attain status for their theological thought by finding
theistic elements or grounds in the Vedas and the Upanishads. By
their general acceptance into the broad sphere of Hindu thought,
theistic conceptions of the Divine were established which did not
support the unknowability of Brahman that was firmly entrenched
in philosophic thought. Thinkers like Shankara saw theism as being,
at best, only a relative knowledge of Brahman, wherein the formed
(*saguna*) Brahman existed to aid men in their ignorance, while the
unformed (*nirguna*) Brahman remained the Absolute beyond the
ignorance (*avidyā*) of man. It remained for the theists, in their religious belief and practice, to find in their particular deity (*Ishvara*)
what for them was the Absolute source and sustenance of their
existence.

Given the Unity and the Order which is inherent to It and the
theistic conviction that the Unity is to be characterized as Deity, a
central concern as to the nature of man remained. We have noted the
fundamental Hindu answer to the question in our brief mention of
Shankara and Ramanuja. The Upanishads, while allowing room for
some variation in the interpretation of their position, had firmly
established for Hindu thought the conviction that there is a relationship between the ultimate Unity and the ultimate essence
(*ātman*) of man. In the case of the two leading philosophical-theological systems, the absolute non-dualism (*Advaita*) of Shankara and
the qualified non-dualism (*Visistadvaita*) of Ramanuja, this relationship was one of an absolute or qualified identity. For Advaita
thought, the soul or ultimate self of man, was identical with the
ultimate Unity in and behind all existence and non-existence. Thus,
Brahman equals Ātman and Ātman equals Brahman. For Visistadvaita this identity was qualified to the extent that, once existing as
a separate though closely related derivative entity, the Ātman maintained individual separateness though, again, always in a position
of close and integral relationship. Ātman proceeds from Brahman,
but ultimately it returns to a condition of intimate relationship,
not absolute identity.

With the exception of a few schools of Indian philosophy, such
as the dualistic Samkhya system,[14] the general philosophical understanding of the ultimate nature of man has followed the Advaita
interpretation. This has also been true for the philosophical and

religious mysticism which is primarily associated with Shankara
and Advaita. In the popular Bhakti religious groups, which are
much more typical of general Hindu religion, the thought of
Ramanuja and the Visistadvaita has generally predominated.
Hinduism, like the other religions we are considering, does not
always teach its adherents the metaphysical presuppositions underlying the most simple of religious beliefs and practices, at least, not
consciously. However, these metaphysical presuppositions, over the
centuries, have influenced the understanding of the nature of man
to such a degree that they have become an integral part of religious
beliefs and practices.

With the foregoing presupposition as to the Ātman and its relation to the Ultimate as a basic theme in Hindu thought, the question remains as to the present condition and predicament of man
in the world of being. Why is the Ātman, though actually the
Brahman, apparently separated from the Brahman and subject to
the problems and limitations of human existence? Or, why is the
Ātman, derived from and closely related to the Brahman, now in a
physical existence in which that relationship is obscured? In each
case there is either an actual separation between the self of man
and the Unity or a radical misunderstanding, an ignorance (*avidyā*),
on the part of the human intellect as to the situation and condition
in which it believes man to be.

A fundamental theme of Hindu thought associated primarily, but
not exclusively, with the system of Shankara, is that the empirical
world discernible by man is a realm which is, by nature, illusory.
It is not actual in the sense that it may be said to be fully Real.
Existence misleads man; it fools him into thinking that it is ultimate
when, in reality, it is derivative. The Hindu doctrine of Maya is
one which has led to much misunderstanding in the West. The
statement that existence is an illusion (*maya*) has appeared to many
westerners to be a contention that, illusion does not exist. This
is not what developed Hindu thought has been maintaining. The
early Hindu thinkers and their philosophic descendants clearly
perceived the fundamental fact of human experience to be that man
has confused the world of existence and its changing, transitory
nature with the ultimate Unity which does not change and is not
transitory. Man deludes himself when he identifies what he ex-

periences with the ultimate state of either himself or the totality of being and non-being. Maya, therefore, is to be understood as illusion in the sense that existence is not to be identified with the Absolute which is both within and beyond all that exists and does not exist.

This presupposition as to the nature of man's environment, which is indicated by the term Maya, has been, and continues to be, basic to Hindu thought. Despite differing philosophical interpretations of it, Hinduism has clearly perceived that, from the perspective of the ultimate self or essence of man, the realm of the physical is subsidiary. At best, the world is a secondary reality not to be confused with the ultimate Reality that is within and behind all. At worst, it is to be recognized as constituting an illusion which drives man into greater ignorance and separates him more firmly from the Ultimate. Man finds himself, therefore, in a situation where he must strive to rise above the limitations of the empirical world of being. He is separated from Reality by a veil which, at most, is quasi-real when compared to the Ultimate.

At this point the Hindu doctrine of Karma is of primary importance. Man is tied to the realm of Maya as a result of his actions and his ignorance of their true nature. All deeds have their consequences, and, since the deeds are performed in the sphere of Maya, their results will be in that realm. The realm of change and flux (*samsāra*) is the stage upon which there is the playing out of the Karma of existence. Man is involved in it by the fact of his humanity, as a consequence of his impulse to action, and his conviction that his actions are ultimate and Real in themselves. And, since it is in the basic nature of man to act and to erroneously identify his total self with his actions, he is caught up in a never ceasing involvement with the realm of Samsāra. How can he escape such entanglement so long as he remains man? And how can he cease to be man when all his powers are obviously those which create further action, with its inevitable demand for present and future existence in the sphere of Samsāra?

Salvation or release (*moksha*) from the world of existence (*samsāra*) to a state or level wherein the limitations of Karma do not apply, is the goal of Hinduism in both its specifically philosophic and its religious aspects. Indian philosophy and Indian religion are united in their ultimate aim of attaining a release from the limited

and restricted realm of existence to the unconditioned and unre-
stricted level of being or non-being, wherein the identity or close
relationship between the Ātman and the Brahman will be a fact
unhampered by the deceptions of Maya and the processes of Samsāra. As a result, Hindu philosophy is religious in character and
Hindu religion a dependent partner with philosophy. And, as we
have indicated, even the schools of Hindu philosophy that include
systems of thought which tend to separate them from the "religious"
aspects of the traditional Hindu philosophy, have succumbed to the
philosophical-theological ethos which surrounds them. Philosophy
is not limited to the concern to understand the nature of existence
and ultimate Reality; it is a search for the salvation of man, a salvation which is finally religious or supra-mundane in character.

As an outcome of the basic themes of Hindu philosophy discussed thus far, a variety of avenues or means for the attainment of
man's release from his present predicament have been constructed
and allowed for in Hinduism. As was suggested in our reference to
the Advaita philosophy associated with Shankara, the unconditioned
state that arises with the "knowledge" or awareness that Brahman
equals Ātman and Ātman equals Brahman, is obtained by a process
of meditation and intuition on the part of the individual who has
cut himself off from the sphere of Samsāra and its concerns. This is
a mysticism which identifies the self of the individual with the ultimate Unity. It is not the attainment of a union but, rather, the
intuitive awareness of a state which already exists. It is the overcoming of the ignorance (*maya*) which leads the self to think itself
a separate and distinct entity and which has caused man to think
himself something other than what he is.

As is true in all cases of religious thought that are designated
as mysticism, it is extremely difficult to indicate the nature of a state
of union between the self of man and the Unity, the source of all
that is. The union is beyond all human categories and means of
expression. At most it can be only faintly indicated by means which
are usually aesthetic in nature. That which is "wholly other" from
all categories of human understanding cannot be put into terms
meaningful to the limited intellect of man. And, also, the final
means for such experience cannot be taught by words or set forth in
clearly defined procedures commensurate with the normal or usual

methods men follow in intellectual development and understanding. The moment of final awareness is not an intellectual one; it is supra-intellectual. It is intuitive in nature in that it involves the whole feeling of the individual, yet physical states and mental attitudes are not the primary factors in the attainment. Awareness of all else but the One Reality is removed, yet the One Reality is now clearly discerned to be *the* All. We shall have to leave to the mystics of all ages and religions the attempt to convey to us the nature of the mystic experience, and they are the first to remind us that the task is an impossible one.[15]

In Hinduism the great mystic path (*Jñāna marga* or *yog*) has been constructed upon the thought expressed in the upanishadic phrase *tat tvam asi*, "That art Thou." When this is understood, or better, perceived, then the limitations of Samsāra are no longer applicable. It is recognized that the inescapable restrictions of Karma are placed upon the external aspects of man; the Ātman does not act and is not acted upon. What man had *thought* to be himself acted, and, as a result of his ignorance, man believed himself to be subject to Karma and its unfolding. In reality, the innermost self (*Pranomaya Ātman*) is beyond Karma. There is no rebirth, no enslavement to the process of Samsara, for the ignorance associated with existence is removed by the recognition of the union of the self and Brahman which has always been the true state of the self. Following the logic of his metaphysical thought, the philosopher has gone beyond philosophy, with its intellectual processes and speculation, to total union with the Absolute.

The theistic philosophical and religious thought of Hinduism has been identified to a large extent, as we noted, with the Bhakti sects. Bhakti has at its base the conviction that man's salvation is to be obtained through the grace of God. While recognizing that the world of being can and does delude man, it has not accepted the extreme Advaita position concerning Maya. For the Bhakti, the Divine appears in the world in the form of incarnations (*avataras*) to serve as guides and teachers of men, and as objects of worship and adoration. Given man's nature, there is nothing he himself can do to escape the consequences of Karma. However, the Adorable One (*Bhagavat*), God (*Ishvara*), bestows release upon those who worship Him or Her in love and adoration. The way of Bhakti is thus open to all who in devout love, trust, and self-surrender, call upon God in humble faith. As a result, the Bhakti cults have developed a worship rich in emotion and color, a worship which calls upon men to turn to God as their one hope for salvation from the iron grip of Karma and the round of rebirths which it imposes. And, the final condition of the soul of man is one in which it finds itself in blessed relationship with the Divine, its source.

A third method or way (*Yog* or *Marga*) of moksha from the unceasing wheel of Samsāra has also been firmly established through the centuries of Hinduism. In fact, it is to be closely identified with the earliest of Hindu religious practice and precedes the rise of Jñāna and Bhakti. This is salvation or release by means of Karma itself. In this case, however, the term Karma is not so much related to the so-termed Law of the Deed as a restrictive force upon man as it is to the conception of the proper deeds and actions which will assure the individual a desired repayment. Since all deeds have their consequences, it follows that acts which are in conformity to the will of an individual deity will effect a desired or beneficial result. By performing proper deeds to favor and please them, by reciting prayers and offering gifts to them, the gods or goddesses, to whom such acts were directed, would give man the reward which was almost automatically demanded by such good Karma. These religious acts and the correct observance of the social duties, incumbent upon one because of the responsibility (*dharma*) of his position in life, assured one of a period in the heaven of the deity following the present life on earth.

The line between each of these three recurring themes concerning moksha is not always clear and distinct. The persistence of the early and more primitive religious practice associated with Karma *yog* has kept it an important part of much of popular Hindu religion. It has mixed with Bhakti and has not totally escaped the philosophical thought produced by Jñāna. For those who have adhered totally to it, there has been little, if any, conscious awareness of the more sophisticated thought associated with the other two. Moksha has been but a temporary matter, a relatively brief escape from earthly existence, when considered in the light of the Hindu understanding of time. But such good Karma is an aid in the preparation for future stages of rebirth which will enable one to reach a higher level of salvation. In its inclusiveness, Hinduism has allowed even that which at first glance appears to be far removed from its highest insights to be included in its total philosophical-theological system. Even though its unsophisticated nature may be highly frowned upon by the philosopher, it is recognized as being of service and value to those who are not able to appreciate the greater truth.

One additional basic theme of Hindu thought must be dealt with in our attempt to discern the recurring elements of Hinduism through the centuries. This is the conception of Avataras which has been referred to briefly. Hindu theism has received its strength and appeal in large measure from the belief in the incarnation of the Divine. Each of the theistic expressions has at its center the conviction that the Divine is available to humanity and, in fact, is concerned with man in the present life and in the future. This divine concern is evidenced by the appearance of incarnations of the Divine among men as teachers and guides; it is demonstrated by the availability of the Divine in various forms as an object of worship and succor.

Each of the Hindu theistic sects has as its object of worship a deity which has incarnated itself in some great figure of the past or which continues to make itself manifest through the medium of saintly and divine figures in the present. Care must be taken here not to succumb to the frequent western error of assuming that all great contemporary Hindu religious figures are conceived as being Avataras. A saintly life may well be a reflection of the Divine; it is not necessarily to be equated with an earthly incarnation of the Divine.

Hinduism, therefore, has readily available to it an understanding of the divine revelation which provides ground for the conviction that the Divine is continually present in the sphere in which men live. The strong tendency of Hindu philosophic speculation to place the concerns of humanity outside the solicitude of the Divine (since they are minor and relative whereas the philosophic Ultimate has no such qualities), is firmly counterbalanced by the religious theism which is central to Hinduism. The Divine appears in many times and in many forms in order that mankind may not be lost and without support.

Each of the basic themes we have mentioned has not only given a philosophical-theological structure to Hinduism in the past, but it has also served as a recurring means for expression of the Hindu religious sensitivity. Rita, Brahman, Dharma, Ātman, Maya, Samsāra, Karma, Moksha, Ishvara, Avatara—these and others have been the foundation upon which Hinduism has been constructed and upon which it continues to rest. They are formalized in the philosophy and in the scholarly literature, they furnish the setting for the popular legends and stories—in short, they are primary factors in the past and present ethos of Hindu India. The Hinduism of the future will only continue to be Hinduism to the degree that these themes and their influence are present.

3

Since early in the nineteenth century, Hindu philosophy and religion have been confronted with an invasion of non-Indian culture which has had far-reaching effect upon Indian life and Hindu thought. During the past two centuries the spread of western thought and culture has proved to be of greater importance than the political and economic expansion of the western powers that it accompanied. The expansion of political and economic power inevitably serves as the vehicle for the extension of the cultural ethos with which the power was initially associated. In some instances the penetration of foreign thought is overt and its success easily determined; in most instances the process is subtle and the results, while discernible, are not easily evaluated.

As the essence of the life and culture of India, Hinduism has borne much of the brunt of the western invasion of the Indian peninsula. While the West has been more aware of the political and social problems of India as a colony and then a new independent nation, those Indians and non-Indians sensitive to the contemporary currents and problems of Indian life have realized that the thought and way of life that is Hinduism has been deeply and inextricably involved in a struggle of survival and in an adaption and regrouping of its forces. While in previous centuries Hinduism had succeeded in maintaining itself as the predominant, though not only, religious and social factor in an India under Muslim control, in the last centuries it has been confronted by a combination of political, economic, social, and technological powers and forces which carried with them a foreign religion and philosophy which sometimes openly, and sometimes subtly, threatened to destroy it.

The Hindu reaction is to be noted particularly in the middle and late decades of the nineteenth century. Young intellectuals, who in some cases had received their higher education under western auspices, began to be vividly aware of the lethargy of Hinduism as a philosophy, religion, and culture. Yet, at the same time they were concerned to overcome the lack of dynamism within Hinduism, they were also convinced of the fundamental truth and value of the Hindu philosophic and religious tradition. They conceived Hinduism to be the proper way of thought and life for India and to be a viable philosophy and religion for the world as a whole. While some were primarily or exclusively concerned with Hinduism for the Hindus, others were beginning to come to the realization that Hinduism possessed the resources and potentiality of being a world philosophy and religion. Hinduism was thus embarked on a venture which has placed it in the midst of the ideologies competing for world recognition and acceptance.

As a result, the concern of Hindu philosophy in recent decades has been to state the themes of Hinduism in a manner which makes clear their relevance to both Hindus and non-Hindus alike. The Hindu intellectual leadership of the immediate past and present has been seeking to fulfill the dual role of teachers at home and proclaimers abroad. Religious leaders and philosophical thinkers have been active in revealing to their own people, particularly the younger educated generation, the depths of Hindu spirituality and intellectual attainment which had been almost forgotten. Interestingly enough, in some cases it has been through books written primarily for western consumption that this awareness has become most acute among the educated Hindus. Some of these thinkers, such as Sri Aurobindo,[16] have been pre-eminently men of religion who have combined their deep religious experience and sensitivity, their awareness of the depth and breadth of modern man's predicament, and their brilliant minds, to present to their fellow men a spiritual philosophy and life of rich attractiveness. Others, such as Professor Radhakrishnan,[17] have been pre-eminently academic philosophers who have brought together their wide knowledge, their brilliant philosophical insight, and their spiritual sensitivity to present to the world the wealth of the "Hindu View of Life."

The process of modern history, therefore, has called Hinduism to a venture far beyond the confines of its long past and varied experience. Rich in tradition, strong in resources, adhered to by brilliant speculative minds—Hindu thought is today a competing partner in the creation of the future actions, beliefs, and allegiances of mankind.

NOTES

[1] H. Zimmer, *Philosophies of India*, edited by J. Campbell (New York: Meridian Books, Inc., 1956), pp. 14-66. A general introductory discussion of philosophy within the Indian context.

[2] Buddha Prakash, "The Hindu Philosophy of History," *Journal of The History of Ideas*, XVI, No. 4, (1955).

[3] Two standard works are:

S. N. Dasgupta, *A History of Indian Philosophy* (5 vols.; Cambridge: Cambridge University Press, 1922-55).

S. Radhakrishnan, *Indian Philosophy* (2nd ed., 2 vols.; London: George Allen & Unwin, Ltd., 1929).

[4] For the layman, a clear and scholarly discussion is found in:

Stuart Piggott, *Prehistoric India* (Baltimore: Penguin Books, Inc., 1950).

See also:

R. D. Bannerji, "Dravidian Civilization," *Modern Review* (Calcutta), September, 1927, pp. 304-14.

———, *ibid.*, November, 1927, pp. 552-59.

W. Norman Brown, "The Beginnings of Civilization in India," *Journal of the American Oriental Society*, LIX, Supp., pp. 32-44.

R. P. Chanda, "Survival of the prehistoric Civilization of the Indus Valley," *Memoirs of the Archaeological Survey of India*, No. 41 (Calcutta, 1929).

V. G. Childe, *The Aryans* (New York: Alfred A. Knopf, Inc., 1926).

D. H. and M. E. Gordon, "Survivals of the Indus Culture," *Journal of the Royal Asiatic Society of Bengal, Letters* (Calcutta, 1940), pp. 66-71.

H. Heras, "The Religion of the Mohenjo-daro People according to the Inscriptions," *Journal of the University of Bombay*, V, pp. 1-29.

P. Joseph, "The Extent and Influence of the Indus Civilization," *Journal of Oriental Research*, (Madras) XI, pp. 246-50.

E. J. H. Mackay, *The Indus Civilization* (London: L. Dickinson & Thompson, 1935).

H. G. Rawlinson and S. V. Venkateswara, "The Indus Valley Civilization: Two Views," *Aryan Path* (Bombay, 1934), pp. 84-90.

[5] A. A. Macdonell, "The Hymn of Creation," *Hymns from the Rigveda* (London: Oxford University Press, 1922), X, 129.

[6] H. D. Griswold, *The Religion of the Rigveda* (London: Oxford University Press, 1923).

A. B. Keith, *The Religion and Philosophy of the Veda and Upanishads* Harvard Oriental Series, XXXI, XXXII (Cambridge: Harvard University Press, 1925).

Louis de La Vallée-Poussin, *Notions sur les religions de l'Inde; Le Védisme* (Paris: Bloud, 1909).

[7] For English translations of the Upanishads, see:

R. E. Hume, *The Thirteen Principal Upanishads* (London: Oxford University Press, 1921). Includes an extremely helpful introduction to upanishadic thought.

Swami Nikhilananda, *The Upanishads* (4 vols.; New York: Harper & Row, Publishers, 1949-60).

Paul Deussen, *Die Philosophie de Upanishads* (Weisbaden: F. A. Brockhaus, 1899). Continues as a classic exposition by a western scholar.

[8] For discussions of Jainism, see:

H. von Glasenapp, *Der Jainismus* (Berlin: Alf Häger, 1925).

J. Jaini, *Outlines of Jainism* (Cambridge: Cambridge University Press, 1916).

Mrs. S. T. Stevenson, *The Heart of Jainism* (London: Oxford University Press, 1915).

[9] T. R. V. Murti, *The Central Philosophy of Buddhism* (London: George Allen & Unwin, Ltd., 1955).

S. Radhakrishnan, *The Dhammapada* (London: Oxford University Press, 1950). Introductory Essay.

[10] Radhakrishnan, *op. cit.*, Vol. II, Chap. VIII. All such general works on Hinduism and Indian philosophy give consideration to Shankara.

More detailed studies of the thought of Shankara are:

P. Deussen, *Outline of the Vedanta System of Philosophy according to Shankara*, trans. J. H. Woods and C. B. Runkel (Cambridge: Harvard University Press, 1927).

V. S. Ghate, *Le Védanta: Étude sur les Brahmasutras et leur cinq Commentaries* (Tours: Imp. E. Arrault, 1918).

Paul Hacker, *Untersuchungen über Texte des frühen Advaitavāda. 1. Die Schüler Sankaras* (Mainz: Akademie der Wissenschaften und der Literatur, 1950).

N. S. Mukharji, *A Study of Sankara* (Calcutta: University of Calcutta, 1942).

K. S. Murty, *Revelation and Reason in Advaita Vedanta* (New York: Columbia University Press, 1959).

R. Otto, *Mysticism East and West* (New York: The Macmillan Company, 1932).

S. Radhakrishnan, *The Vedanta According to Sankara and Ramanuja* (London: George Allen & Unwin, Ltd., 1924).

R. P. Singh, *The Vedanta of Sankara—a Metaphysics of Value* (Jaipur: Bharat Publishing House, 1949).

[11] R. G. Bhandarkar, *Vaisnavism, Saivism and Minor Religious Systems* (Stassburg: Trubner, 1913).

Ghate, *op. cit.*

N. Macnicol, *Indian Theism* (London: Oxford University Press, 1915).

R. Otto, *India's Religion of Grace and Christianity* (New York: The Macmillan Company, 1930).

S. Radhakrishnan, *Indian Philosophy*, Vol. II, Chap. IX.

———, *The Vedanta According to Sankara and Ramanuja.*

K. C. Varadachari, *Sri Ramanuja's Theory of Knowledge* (Tirupati: Tirumalai-Tirupati Devasthanams Press, 1943).

[12] Bhandarkar, *op. cit.*, this remains the most scholarly one volume treatment of the thought and leadership of such religious movements. See also individual studies such as:

W. S. Deming, *Rāmdās and the Rāmdāsīs* (London: Oxford University Press, 1928).

W. G. Orr, *A Sixteenth Century Indian Mystic* (London: Lutterworth, 1947).

[13] For interpretive discussions of the Bhagavad-Gita, see:

Franklin Edgerton, *The Bhagavad Gītā* (Cambridge: Harvard University Press, 1944), II, 37-92.

S. Radhakrishnan, *The Bhagavadgītā* (New York: Harper & Row, Publishers, 1948), pp. 11-78.

[14] A. B. Keith, *The Sāmkhya System* (London: Oxford University Press, 1918). Zimmer, *op. cit.*, pp. 280-332.

[15] W. T. Stace, *Mysticism and Philosophy* (Philadelphia: J. B. Lippincott Company, 1960), especially Chap. 6. A discussion of the problem by a leading contemporary philosopher.

[16] Aurobindo Ghose (1872-1950) was a unique, and yet in a sense not untypical Hindu, combination of the East and the West, and the political and spiritual. Born in India, educated in England from the age of seven to twenty-one, he spent his early adult years in governmental service and Indian political activity. At thirty-eight he turned completely to the life of the Hindu mystic-philosopher and for a period of forty years served as a leading thinker and spiritual leader of modern India. His influence has by no means ceased since his death. See especially: *The Life Divine* (3rd ed., 2 vols.; Calcutta: Ayra Publishing House, 1947).

[17] The president of India, formerly Spalding Professor of Eastern Religions and Ethics at Oxford University, occupant of many distinguished academic positions in India, Sarvepalli Radhakrishnan has served as Hindu philosophy's most eloquent spokesman to the West and as the inspiration of the newer generations of Hindu intellectuals. See previous references to his many writings, and: *The Hindu View of Life* (London: George Allen & Unwin, Ltd., 1927).

IV
The
Teaching
of
Buddhism

The beginnings, early development, and later flowering of Buddhism constitute an unfolding chronicle that includes a partnership with the leading cultures of Asia. From its Indian origins through its varied migrations to its present position as a primary element in eastern culture as a whole, Buddhism has succeeded in establishing itself as a way of life and of belief which serves as a uniting factor among the Asian peoples. To consider Buddhism is to consider the greater part of Asia and its history. To ignore Buddhism is to ignore not only the religion but the cultural ethos which has served to create much of the Asian world-view down to the present day.

Within a few centuries of its origin, Buddhism demonstrated itself to be a religion not to be limited to a specific culture or form of society. Arising as a protest against a particular religious-social-philosophical system, it has proceeded during its history to associate itself with a variety of systems. In each of these alliances Buddhism has been required to make adjustments to indigenous traditions which have, in turn, been forced to bring themselves in line with the essentials which constitute the historic character of Buddhism. There are few religions in world history which demonstrate a greater adaptability to new circumstances than Buddhism; there are few which under the necessity of circumstance have synthesized themselves in like degree with foreign ingredients. Whether this process of adaption has in its cultural and geographic expansion brought about the dilution of the initial religious insights of Buddhism, is a question debated by its critics and rejected by its defenders. Despite its great variety of forms and its proliferation of expressions, it has maintained a common body of presuppositions which gives it a ground of unity beneath its wide diversity.

In its conception Buddhism, as we have noted, was one of the great Indian protests against the religious rigidity of the Brahmanism of the middle and late centuries of the first millennium B.C. Greatly indebted to many of the central themes of the Hindu thought of the period, Buddhism, along with Hinduism, has continued to depend upon them as the foundation pillars upon which its philosophy has been erected. Violently protesting, then and later, against other themes essential to Hindu philosophy, Buddhism has in many of its expressions incorporated those elements into itself in the course of its own pilgrimage. Always Indian in a sense, Buddhism has found its spheres of greatest influence beyond India. Despite the non-Indian influences which have done much to make it what it is today, there still remains within all Buddhist groups a core of thought which was Indian in origin, Indian in early development, Indian in its form of expressions, and Indian in its understanding of existence.

Throughout its history Buddhism has found itself in a dialectical realtionship with other religions and cultures. Its early experience of more than a thousand years in the Hindu context was to be duplicated throughout the Far East. Entering into areas where other religions were predominant for the most part, Buddhism was confronted with the need to establish itself within advanced cultures which had traditional associations with indigenous religions that were naturally opposed to the new rival. The dynamic appeal of Buddhism enabled it to become a vital and paramount element in the new areas. This success, however, was not without adjustment by Buddhism, an adaption to new circumstances which carried with it inevitable enrichment and impoverishment of the earlier content of its message.

In the process of its wide geographic advance, the religion that had begun in north India became a religion which both retained and lost its Indian nature. There are few Christians who would regret that early Christianity ventured beyond its Jewish beginnings, though many have wished that the community and teachings of the early Apostolic period might be regained. For Buddhism the situation is much the same. The experience of the two religions is analogous in the degree to which both early declared their independence of their religious forerunners. Because of their further declaration of the unlimited nature of their mission, both have been subjected to the tensions which inevitably arise as new cultures and foreign thought-worlds are encountered. In the adaptions they have been required to make, and the new modes of thought incorporated, they have taken into themselves elements with the potential to destroy their initial *raison d'etre*. Scholars will continue to be intrigued as to whether each of them has, through historical necessity, been diluted or enriched by the process. Buddhism, when seen in its totality, has obviously expanded the content of its message and varied the method of its expression.

In each case of adjustment to new surroundings, Buddhism demonstrated itself to be prepared to take the local environment and its traditions into account. This is not to contend that it did not oppose the indigenous religions which it confronted; it is, however, to suggest that it proved itself to be flexible in its approach and tolerant in its views. From the perspective of the western observer, this general tolerance on the part of Buddhism resulted in a synthesis with the local cults and national religions, with the consequence that Buddhism became less an international religion and more a collection of local religions each somewhat distinct from the other. From the perspective of the Buddhist, this adaptability is conclusive proof of the universal suitability of Buddhism as the vehicle of salvation for all mankind.

In approaching a discussion of Buddhism, it is essential that we remind ourselves of the historic nature of its initial beginnings and the relationship of this historic event to the subsequent Buddhist understanding of the religion. It must be understood that Buddhism differs from Hinduism in its consciousness of an historic event and an historic person. Because of the emphasis upon history which is associated with the Semitic religions best known to the West, westerners have put Hinduism and Buddhism together as religions which place no real emphasis upon history. It is true that both the eastern religions do have a different conception of history and that this difference is of great significance for their philosophical expressions. However, in the case of Buddhism, this difference is misunderstood if it causes oversight of the central importance of the Person and experiences of the historic Buddha, Siddhatta Gotama. We shall refer to his religious experience and teachings in a later context, but at this point the importance of his role for the development of early Buddhism and subsequent Buddhist philosophical systems must be stressed. Non-Buddhists are all too eager to point to the degree to which the historic Buddha is overshadowed by the supra-mundane Buddhas central to much of the developed religion; they are forgetful that because of its historic beginnings in an historic person Buddhism has an appreciation of human history which gives that history a meaning and content easily overlooked. The point is a difficult one, and the ramifications and exceptions many; nevertheless it must be reckoned with if Buddhism is to be understood.

One further matter must be considered by way of introduction. Each of the great religions of the contemporary world has had, and continues to have, its divisions, its sects, its different schools of theological or philosophical interpretation. Buddhism shares in this condition. Its division into the two great groups of the Theravada, or Hinayana as it is usually known in the West, and the Mahayana is generally known to many. What is often forgotten is that within these two groups there are still many varying groupings, each of which considers itself to be the preferable or correct understanding of Buddhism. Each has its own beginnings and traditions, its own most important literature, its own philosophical expressions of the Buddhist religious message. In Theravada, or southern Buddhism, there are varying schools of philosophical thought and differing cultural understandings of the religious life, though a general unity runs through them all. In Mahayana or northern Buddhism similar factions exist and are, in fact, more numerous. Each understands itself to be related to the original experience which gave birth to Buddhism. It will be part of our task to discover the unity in the midst of the variety and to ascertain the significant themes of contemporary Buddhism as it continues to seek to be a universal religion.

1

We have previously noted the general religious and philosophical situation in India in the sixth century B.C. and have also referred to the rise of Buddhism and Jainism as protests within that context. However, it must be remembered that protests are to be viewed from two perspectives—that against which the protest is raised and the content of the protest's expression. The first is negative, the second potentially positive. In the instance of those religious protests which have continued beyond the initial period of their objection and gone on to become influential religions in their own right, the positive element, not the negative, has been the distinctive character of the protest. Some movements have their origin predominantly as protests, and their new or positive content is itself negative in nature. Their dynamic rises from the truth and intensity of their objections; it disappears as the undesirable is overcome or forgotten. Other movements come into being as a result of experience, insight, and conviction which is held to be true because of its own intrinsic value. The dynamic here is the product of new belief to which deep commitment is given. The negative protest is secondary, if even acknowledged. The protest may supply fuel for the flame. It does not become the flame itself.

The beginnings of Buddhism are to be understood in this light. If they are not, the initial dynamic and the continued appeal of Buddhism to men remain a mystery. Buddhism had its origin in the positive personal experience of its historic founder. It has continued to have meaning as a result of the positive values it bestows in and through the personal experiences of men and women.

The traditional account of the life and teachings of the Buddha will likely be known to the readers of these pages. It presents a young man born under miraculous circumstances to wealth and noble position and purposefully points to the worldly enjoyments and luxurious surroundings available to him. It notes his growing discontent with such pleasures, his sensitivity to the inequities and sufferings which are the lot of mankind, and, in devoted admiration, chronicles his abrupt turning from a life of shallow concerns

to an intensive search for fundamental truth. The trials and sufferings of that search serve to remind the devout Buddhist of the rigors
of the sincere religious quest. And while, for the moment, we shall
disregard the more serious aspects of whether the Buddha's great
experience and early teaching were "religious" or not, we would
insist that his painful path of searching, which culminated in the
experience, was fully religious within the Indian context of the
time and the experience of men throughout history. It was intellectual; it was meditative; it was intuitive; it was religious. A definition
of religion which would exclude the trying pilgrimage of the Buddha to his moment of great enlightenment, would be one which
grievously misunderstands both that particular striving and the
nature of religion in human experience.

Following the custom of his day and place, the Buddha sought
by means of ascetic denial to free himself from the sufferings which
are the lot of man. He endeavored to find in the subjection of the
body the fulfillment of the self. Gaining some fame for his ascetic
diligence, he knew that his attainment was an empty one. He was
not free from earthly bondage and its engulfing entanglements. He
had substituted one way of life for another, and, though the circumstances of living were now different, the ultimate concerns which
held his attention were not dissimilar. Sincerely and fully submit-
ting himself to the accepted Indian methods of physical living and
intellectual speculation and meditation, the Buddha found each of
them to be incomplete and ultimately valueless, since the reasons
for his pilgrimage remained, and his sensitivity to their tragic and
inescapable nature was heightened, not decreased, by his quest.

It was at this point of realization, of awareness that the accepted
religious strivings of men lead all too easily to emphasis upon the
striving with a resulting loss of the goal which is sought, that the
Buddha received the enlightenment (*Bodhi*) which marked the beginning of Buddhism. Seated in meditation, a consciousness, a
knowledge, an insight of revelation that transcended all intellectual
processes, became his. As later Buddhism was to claim, and modern
Buddhists insist, this experience was not anti-intellectual; it was
supra-intellectual. Enlightenment which brings truth to men is an
experience wherein the full resources of the intellect are required
and yet they are transcended.

From this moment there was now available to mankind the means whereby striving might cease, the limitations of human existence overcome, and the ultimate fulfillment of men be attained. The means had been brought into the sphere of human history, and history could not be the same from that time on. The event had happened within *this* Age, and, from the occurence of the event onward, a new hope and assurance were available to lift men beyond the confines to which human history had been limited.

It is essential to an understanding of the warmth of Buddhism, and of the place of the earthly Buddha in the affections of Buddhists, that we give attention to the struggle of the Buddha which tradition records immediately after he himself had received the enlightenment which constituted his experience. An essential element of the enlightenment was the release it brought from earthly attachment. Did this mean, then, that the Buddha himself was to be free from concern for those who, unlike himself, had not received freedom? Was his experience to be one that removed him from all sensitivity to those anguishing problems which had first motivated his religious struggle and continued to contribute to the despair of men? Had the enlightenment occurred but once, for him only, to pass away without the notice of others? Or were the values of the enlightenment which had come to him, and were now the essence of his own Person, applicable to men within the context of their historical, earthly lives? The answer to this question gives us one of the most significant clues to the character of Buddhism and the dynamic of its message to men. The man who sought his own salvation and found it in an experience which told him in part that concern for earthly existence was a primary barrier to salvation, became the Compassionate Buddha who sought to serve his earthly brothers as their teacher and their guide. The Buddha's understanding of the relevance of his experience for all mankind, and the subsequent undertaking of his earthly ministry, thus became a foremost happening in human history.

The ministry began in a fashion not unlike that which was traditional within Indian religious history. A man had discovered a path to release from the Karma and the Samsāra which dooms mankind to rebirth. Those who were prepared to embark upon his difficult path came to hear and to learn the secret for themselves. However, there was something different in this teacher and his message. The way was open to all. No man was restricted by his birth; no man was forbidden because of his occupation or his lack of conformance to a cultic or social tradition. Elements which in the preaching of later Indian saints were not uncommon, in the preaching of the Buddha were largely unique and new. A community of adherents came into being, a group which from that time on was to constitute the nucleus for the growing number of witnesses to the relevance of the experience of the Buddha for all mankind. Until the end of his long earthly life the Buddha spent his time in instructing those who came to him. And not least among his teachings was the injunction that they were to preach it to others.

The teachings of the Buddha reflect the close relationship with, and dependence of Buddhism upon, the basic philosophical orientation of the India of his time. This metaphysical world-view was fundamental to the enlightenment which released the Buddha from his quest. It served as a foundation upon which the path to enlightenment could be preached, and it constituted the framework in which the message of the preaching, though different, could be understood.

First and foremost, the message of early Buddhism was one which rested upon the Hindu understanding of the inexorable nature of causality (*karma*) which is related to all things, their constitution, and the events in which they are involved. All things have their prior cause, and each cause is related to an antecedent which in turn is dependent in origin. This, which up to this time had been accepted as fact by Indian thinkers, was made explicit and clear in the preaching of the Buddha and in the philosophical systems created by his leading followers. Given this understanding of the fundamental nature of being, all interpretations of being, its nature and characteristics, must take into account this law and its ramifications.

The Buddha proclaimed to his hearers that his enlightenment, while of a nature beyond human capability of conception, was an experience in which it was made clear that all life, all existence, all being, was at base a state which involved suffering (*dukkha*). This suffering—actually all of being—is the result of a preceding cause. The Law of Dependent Origination operates here as in all things and events. It is here that it is to be discerned by sensitive men most clearly, and it is here that it acts to circumscribe and bind men most effectively. The enlightenment of the Buddha authenticated the truth of Dependent Origination as the primary factor in empirical existence. Men may speculate about, may affirm or deny, cause and effect. Enlightenment establishes it.[1]

The experience of the Buddha, and the next step in his message, was that existence itself, which is composed of suffering, is the effect of desire. It is desire that is at the root of man's being and its inherent nature of sorrow. The thirst for things, for a state or states of being, for pleasure, for power, for all that constitutes being—it is this desire, thirst, drive which brings about the condition we know as existence, and the resulting suffering which is its nature. Suffering does not arise by itself; it is not solely inherent in existence because to exist is to suffer. To exist is to suffer because to exist is to be in a state of desire, of thirst after existence and all its potential forms.

The message of the Buddha, and the core of his preaching, was that there was a way, a path, whereby the root cause of suffering, namely desire, could be overcome. After his own enlightenment he had returned to men to preach to them the Law (*Dhamma*)[2] which, if accepted and followed, would also eventually lead them to enlightenment, to release in which desire and its effects would cease. If suffering results from desire, is contingent upon it, then it is obvious that there can be no hope of removing suffering unless it is possible to eradicate desire. And the good news of Buddhism was the revelation to men that such overcoming of desire is possible. As a testimony on earth to its feasibility and its joyous results, it had been accomplished by one who lived among them.

The overcoming of desire is possible to man through the following of the path which the Buddha preached. It is a path which consists of eight steps or elements, a Middle Path between a rejection of the world and an extreme indulgence in it. The first three of the Noble Truths—suffering, desire, and the former as an inevitable result of the latter—are shown to be potentially temporary, though long in past duration, if men turn in full commitment to the Noble Eightfold Path which is the crown of the Buddha's message to all mankind. This, the fourth of the Noble Truths, is the means whereby man is released from the Law of Dependent Origination, from the Karma which chains him to the world of Samsāra and suffering. Right view, right resolution, right speech, right action, right livelihood, right effort, right mindfulness, and right concentration—following the Path of these eight disciplines will lead man to the enlightenment which will authenticate the Gospel of Buddhism in a realm of non-being (*Nibbana*), where there is no desire, no sorrow, no Dependent Origination. Existence or phenomena (*nama-rupa*), in the sense in which the human intellect perceives such categories, will be transcended; they will not be, and neither will they not not be. Nibbana, the ineffable, is the destiny of those who have the courage to fully commit themselves to the Middle Path of the Buddha.

The foregoing was the essential character of the earthly preaching of the Buddha. And though on the surface it appears simple, certainly not complex if the basic presuppositions of Hindu philosophy at the time are accepted, it was to serve as the basis for philosophical-theological speculation and system building which has attracted the attention and devotion of multitudes of scholars from the time of the Buddha until today.[3] Beginning as a pronouncement of a way to release, it flowered into a code of earthly conduct, a method of intellectual endeavor, a system of metaphysical speculation and belief, and a way of religious worship. Exciting and attractive to the intensely rigorous philosopher, it nevertheless appealed to the religiously sensitive. Promising release from the burdens of life which weigh upon all men, it met their needs at whatever level was their lot.

The early Buddhist community was primarily a monastic one. The requirements of the Middle Path were rigorous in nature. They demanded a commitment which would not allow an individual the opportunity to continue in the normal life of the householder, with responsibility for a family and the usual social obligations. Men were called upon to devote themselves fully to the Path, and such devotion enjoined an allegiance to the community of fellow seekers which precluded any other social loyalties.[4] Those who were not prepared to make such a commitment but did desire to adhere to the teachings, were allowed a place which made them a part of Buddhism. It did not, however, bring them into the inner circle of the faithful who were now, in this life, fully embarked on the Middle Path to enlightenment.

The monastic community (*Sangha*) soon found itself facing difficulties in the preservation of the Law as it had been given by the Buddha. The complexity of the more subtle teachings of the Master and the ease with which those teachings might be interpreted in different ways by brilliant minds, combined to present the early Sangha with the need to arrive at definitive statements concerning the Law. The result was a series of Councils during the early centuries of Buddhist history. These early Councils served to establish the pattern of Buddhism during its first stages of development, to canonize the early literature, and to give a continuing unity within the already rising variety of Buddhist thought and practice.

The content and discipline of the message of Buddhism was extremely conducive to diversity. The basic tenets necessary to the teaching were established and generally agreed upon; however, the individual character of each man's pilgrimage along the Middle Path inevitably contributed to the rise of individual and group interpretations of procedure and belief which differed from that of other individuals and groups. Rival monastic schools or centers were established around the teachings of exceptionally brilliant and saintly monks (*bhikkhus*); separate traditions were created which were to lead to differing emphases that have continued down through the centuries.

The most important early Buddhist literature, the Three Baskets (*Tipitaka*), is composed of three collections or Books dealing with Buddhist discipline (*Vinaya-pitaka*), the discourses of teachings of the Buddha (*Sutta-pitaka*), and the doctrine or Law (*Abhidhamma-pitaka*). They were essential to the ordering of the life, the intellectual speculation and discipline, and the inspiration of the monks. They were influential in structuring the monastic order and served as a basis for the general understanding of Buddhism among the laity or non-monastic adherents of the faith. The Tipitaka has continued down through the history of Buddhism as a collection of the central core of Buddhist teachings, particularly among southern or Theravada Buddhists. The northern, Mahayanist, expression of Buddhism has gone far beyond the Tipitaka in its understanding of the Law and places greater emphasis upon other scriptures. Nevertheless, it too owes much to the Tipitaka.

The catalogue of Buddhist literature is enormous, and the variety of thought expressed is large. Beyond the Tipitaka and the various records or biographies of the Buddha, the literature is composed for the most part of teachings ascribed to the Buddha by different schools of thought and systematic commentaries on those teachings by the great philosophers of Buddhist history. Most of these reveal a logic and subtlety of thought which is truly brilliant; many indulge in legend and fantasy which gives them a supra-mundane flavor of a religious, rather than a philosophical, nature. Some, such as the Dhammapada,[5] rank among the greatest of the world's wisdom literature; others, such as the Saddharma-pundarika,[6] are to be numbered with the most beautiful apocalyptic writings of all time. Some serve as the individual particular authority and dynamic of separate Buddhist groups; collectively, though many of them are little recognized by some groups, they constitute a preservation and a flowering of the Buddhist teaching.

Within a few centuries following the death of the Buddha, the divergences in interpretation of the Doctrine and in the conception of the Person of the Buddha led to a serious breach in the unity of the Buddhist community. The variety of interpretation, which we have previously mentioned, was largely confined to the monastic community. However, there was a growing division of intellectual thought, as well as the development of divergent concerns for what may more properly be termed religious worship. Buddhism was both limited and strengthened by its monasticism. It was limited in that the sense of intimate participation in the community was not given to the adherents outside the monastic orders. It was strengthened by the degree to which these orders demanded discipline and attention to the learning of the Doctrine and the striving toward enlightenment.

This emphasis upon the Sangha and its monastic character did not give Buddhism the close relationship with the masses of the people which was demanded by its own concern for mankind. It left them religiously in a vacuum. Attracted by its teachings and by the Person of the first teacher, they were left outside the intellectual excitement and endeavor which constituted so much of its dynamic.

And, since it was at most only quasi-religious in that it did not furnish men with a divine object to be worshiped, the religious needs and aspirations of the laity were not met. This contributed to the growth within Buddhism of popular religious practices and beliefs which were not inherent to the early teaching or present in the earliest community.

The development of this religious aspect to Buddhism was aided, and made meaningful within the context of the Doctrine, by the growing separation within the Sangha itself over the question as to the nature of the Person of the Buddha. It is evident that early Buddhism, and the Buddha himself, considered the Buddha to be a human being who had by his own efforts attained true enlightenment. The Buddhist teaching was atheistic in that it did not concern itself with the existence or non-existence of an ultimate divine Being or God. Accepting the general Hindu belief in the existence of supra-mundane beings—gods—it did not hold them to be of significant consequence to the life of man or his escape from the tribulations of life. Gods, too, were the results of Dependent Origination; they were in a predicament not unlike that which confronts man.

Since the gods are no better off, if as well, as man in the total cosmic scheme of things, and since there is no Absolute God, Being, or Essence, it follows then that the Buddha himself was like any living creature. He was a man resulting from Dependent Origination as do all men. He was unlike other men, not in his essential nature as such, but only in that he had by his own efforts attained enlightenment and its resulting freedom from the working of cause and effect. He was a man and not a god, a man to be honored for his attainment, but not worshiped, since there is no need that men do anything other than apply themselves diligently to the Middle Path he has revealed to them.

Such a view toward the founder of a system of belief concerning the nature of existence and man's condition, when combined with the absence in the system itself of an object, or objects, to be worshiped, is not conducive to the development of adherence on the part of the non-intellectual masses of men. The beliefs may be true, but their existential imperative is seldom grasped.

The religious longing and need of the average layman first expressed itself within the context of the new beliefs through the growing adoration and homage that was paid to the Buddha himself. It was supported by the ingrained habit of the laity to turn to those men and deities who were beyond the restrictions of earthly life, either because of their initial nature as deities or their attained stature as beings who were now free. The mind that is not given to intense intellectual activity and speculation, that does not seek full consistency with all aspects of its own presuppositions, is not usually aware of the contradictions into which it falls. Both the laity and many of the Sangha brought with them into Buddhism the religious traditions which were a part of their cultural environment and an essential need to their understanding of existence.

The general tolerant attitude of Buddhism allowed the development within the lay community of cultic acts which, for the layman, made Buddhism a religion and not only a philosophy of life. As a result the history of Buddhism, since early in its development, has been one wherein much of the indigenous religion of the countryside has been synthesized into a Buddhist framework. The pantheons of local deities, the cultic worship, the sometimes subtle religiosity of the culture, the custom morality—all of these have come to find their place or continuation in some form or other within the larger Buddhist metaphysics and teaching concerning ultimate release from the confines of Dependent Origination. The intellectual bhikkhu of the monastery has sometimes disassociated himself from these religious elements of the larger historically developed Buddhism; he has seldom escaped completely from its influence. In everyday Theravada Buddhism, the Buddha has become an object of adoration little short of deification, if it is possible to make such a distinction at all in regard to the thought and practice of the laity. In Mahayana Buddhism, the Buddha has become one among other deities who, at different levels of cosmic existence, seek to bring living creatures into a condition of freedom from earthly limitations. In the former, the philosophy which is associated with it will usually deny the propriety of such a lifting of the earthly Buddha to divine status, though it will accord to him an importance which tends to make him of more significance than all other beings within the cosmos. The latter has in almost all its systems emphasized his divine nature, while at the same time recognizing the Divine to be of such a complex and varied unity that it has, in fact, relegated the earthly Buddha to a comparatively low level in the hierarchy of manifestations of the Divine.

In our subsequent consideration of the essential themes of Buddhism as a philosophy and a religion, it will be necessary for us to divide our discussion in order to indicate the differences of belief and emphasis between the Theravada and Mahayana expressions of historic and contemporary Buddhism. Our brief references to them so far have served to indicate that they constitute the two great traditional representatives of Buddhism and its variations.[7] Within the two classifications are groups which differ widely among themselves in their philosophy and in their cultic forms. The Theravada has become the paramount factor in the history of the culture, philosophy, and religion of southeast Asia; the Mahayana has served the same function and attained the same status among the various highly developed indigenous cultures of the north and eastern areas of Asia.

The first thousand years of Buddhism were marked by the appearance of a number of outstanding philosophers who contributed greatly to the intellectual development and expression of Buddhism. In his own way, each of these thinkers sought to give clear expression to the basic elements of the Law which had been revealed in the teachings of the Buddha. Emphasizing as it did the supra-intellectual, yet intellectual, character of the Buddha's pioneering discovery, Buddhism was forced by its own inherent nature to seek to demonstrate the rational cogency of its teaching. This resulted in the production of literature abounding in the logical analysis which from the beginning was typical of Buddhist philosophical discourse. This literature served to create a tradition of intellectual and dialectical procedure that continues to give Buddhist philosophy an analytical flavor and precision.

This is illustrated in the famous *Milinda-pañha* attributed to the philosopher Nagasena.[8] In the course of a dialogue between the King Milinda and the philosopher Nagasena, it is made clear that the doctrine of the non-permanence of the self (*Anatmavada*) is a result of an analysis of existence commensurate with established principles of logic. By straightforward questions and direct and subtle answers, the Milinda-pañha impresses upon the reader not only the intellectual validity of this important doctrine of the Law but also the necessity that the person seeking enlightenment submit all presuppositions and assumptions he may hold to rigorous investigation. Man cannot easily trust all sense perceptions, nor can he accept without question the systems of interpretation of such perceptions which he constructs in his attempt to understand phenomena and their interrelationships. And, according to Nagasena's demonstration in the Milinda-pañha, such rigorous intellectual investigation will establish that a permanent ultimate essence of a thing, or a self, is not possible.

Another important thinker in the development of Buddhist philosophy, as it is expressed in Pali literature was Buddhaghosa who is outstanding as a literary artist and a philosopher. Writing in the fifth century, A.D., Buddhaghosa produced voluminous works and commentaries which combined to systematize much of the Buddhist philosophy associated with the Theravada tradition. His philosophic acumen and encyclopedic knowledge of Buddhist thought demonstrates to readers today the high form of intellectual sophistication typical of the scholarly Buddhism of the time. His attempts to reconstruct the historical activities of the Buddha and some of his disciples in the *Manorathapūraṇī* and his references to his own activities, particularly in the *Mahāvaṃsa,* have been useful and intriguing to modern scholars in their historical studies of early Buddhism. His *Visuddhi-Magga* assures him a pre-eminent place in the history of Buddhist thought.[9]

In the writings of the scholars of the early Indian development of Sanskrit Buddhist literature, we discern the growing gulf between the two primary trends of philosophy-theology which we now know as Theravada and Mahayana. For example, the creations of the philosopher-poet, Aśvaghosa, particularly his *Buddhacarita,*[10] put forth a highly idealized life of the Buddha and emphasize a devotion and adoration to the Buddha which reveals the growing Buddhology that was to characterize the developing Mahayana Buddhist thought.

The nature of the rapidly flowering Mahayana thought and indications of its philosophic resourcefulness, are revealed in the writings of one of the truly great philosophers of all time, Nāgārjuna. Studying and teaching primarily in south India in the second century A.D., he was the champion of the Mādhyamika (Śūnyavāda) school of philosophy claimed by many scholars to be the primary philosophy in the further development and structuring of Mahayana thought. There are few writings in the field of philosophy which surpass his *Mādhyamika-kārikā* in adherence to a self-imposed rule of logic and few which embark upon a more rigorous search for the ultimate nature of the cosmos. Nāgārjuna was instrumental in charting the path of metaphysical speculation which continues to this day among some of the leading Mahayana schools of philosophy.[11]

Also of primary importance, in creating the basic philosophical framework for subsequent Mahayana development and in their contributions to the early great period of Buddhist philosophy, the brothers Asaṅga and Vasubandhu are to be ranked high in the lists of the world's great philosophers. Writing in the fourth century, Asaṅga established by his works the thought identified with the Yogācāra (Vijñānavāda) school of Buddhist philosophy. His *Yogācāra-bhūmiśāstra* and *Mahāyāna-sūtrālaṅkāra* stabilized the position of the Yogācāra school and gave a basis for the speculation associated with it in subsequent centuries.[12] Vasubandhu, while later identifying himself with the same Mahayana philosophical school as his brother, is known today primarily for his *Abhidharma-kośa* written while he was still associated with the non-Mahayana Sarvāstivāda school. This work has been the subject of a large amount of commentaries written by other Buddhist scholars over the centuries.[13]

In the expansion of Buddhism in both of its major forms into lands far removed from its origin, untold numbers of scholars performed essential work in the translation of earlier writings into native languages, in writing commentaries upon them, and in producing their own systems of philosophy and interpretation. Buddhism became the means for a literary, philosophic, and cultural flowering which brought to the fore the production of the best minds of the peoples involved. And in the process, while Buddhism ceased to be only Indian and became a complex of many cultures, the cultures discontinued their absolute identification with their provincial heritages to become a mixture of their own traditions and Buddhism.

The history of Buddhism from the beginning of the Christian era has been one of expansion out of India and final decay, and almost complete disappearance, within India. By the seventh century, Buddhism in India was showing signs of a decay which in the next few hundred years was to bring about its removal as a religion of real influence within the Indian subcontinent. It was in Ceylon, Burma, Thailand, and adjacent areas that Theravada Buddhism was to find its home and area of continuing influence. These peoples found in Theravada the vehicle for their own selfconsciousness as a society and a culture. Today they are continuing to discover in Theravada a meaningful means for their adjustment to the contemporary problems which confront them. Recognizing its past values and its potential contributions to the present, they are in the midst of a Theravada renaissance which they are convinced promises strength for themselves and others in the present and near future.

Mahayana, after a migration which ended in its firm association with nations and peoples much further removed from its Indian homeland, found its future primarily among the Chinese, Koreans, and Japanese. Here it was to be confronted by indigenous religions and systems of thought which, in some instances, were sharply in contrast with its own early formulations of belief and its inherited organizational patterns. In the centuries since its invasion into these originally foreign areas, it succeeded in either absorbing portions of their traditions into itself, in supplanting them in the affections of the people, or in winning a place alongside them as an acceptable religion and philosophy of life. In all cases Mahayana has attained status as a primary cultural force within the societies of northern and eastern Asia. It has continued within the present century to be the one predominant cultural feature of the area as a whole.

The many centuries of Buddhist history, the great multiplication of its divisions of thought and emphasis, the rich proliferation of literature which it has produced, the resources it has developed for philosophical and metaphysical speculation, the artistic expressions which have accompanied it in all areas, the synthesis it has achieved with the many and varied cultures of Asia, the scholars and religious geniuses who have led it to intellectual and spiritual attainments of high order, the ethical, moral, and religious guidance it has given to generations of Asians, all of these combine to create a story going far beyond its Indian origin. The experience of enlightenment which freed the earthly Buddha from the limitations of existence, and the compassion that caused him to preach the Middle Path to suffering humanity, have together served to change the character of men and societies, both ancient and modern. Whether it shall continue to fulfill this function in the present and the future is, in large part, the burden of Buddhist philosophy.

2

The fundamental and recurring themes of Buddhist philosophical-theological thought have been either explicitly mentioned or implicitly referred to in our discussion of the beginnings and growth of Buddhism. The history of religious and philosophical movements is not simply a chronicle of events which surround them and shape their course in society. Because they are inherently matters of thought and belief as well as organs for action and association, they and their individual histories are understood only when they are discerned as a collection of integrated presuppositions and intellectual commitments which are also subject to influences from their surroundings. These beliefs are expressed in the context of historical events, and, as long as they are esteemed worthwhile by their adherents, they undergo the processes, hazards, and enrichments of historical development.

This is extremely significant in the development of the central themes of Buddhism. Until not many decades ago western scholars were under the impression that the essence of Buddhism, and the significant values of its thought, were to be found primarily in the literature, philosophy, and ethics associated with its earliest history. This view was in part the result of the sequence in which they had become acquainted with Buddhist philosophy; it was, also, the inevitable consequence of the conviction that the essential nature of a religion or philosophy is best discovered in the earliest formulations of its thought. This conviction is not without merit, but its fatal weakness is that it overlooks the ability and need of such phenomena to continue to strive to express their essentials more clearly as time passes and as new understandings of the original experience and insight arise. It does not take into account the obvious fact that the passage of time gives opportunity for more intense application to the meaning of the essential themes; nor does it recognize the important role played by the circumstances of historical variety in bringing forth the richness and depth of these elements which constitute the *raison d'etre* of the religion or philosophy in question. Investigation of the earliest sources undoubtedly reveal earlier understandings on the part of adherents; they do not necessarily enlighten later generations in their search for the meaning and strength of the beliefs. Historical process may very likely produce a diminution or perversion of the original insight; it does not of necessity destroy the essential value which that insight, changed or not, has for men in differing environmental circumstances.

Recognizing that Buddhism has undergone the process of historical change and development, we shall seek to focus our attention upon the essential themes which were present in its earliest formulations of its thought as well as the interpretations and additions to these themes which have been produced over the long period of Buddhist history. Buddhism today is composed of much more than the record of the Buddha's teaching and the early commentaries and enlargements upon it. The themes have been both preserved and ignored, added to and rejected within the divisions of Buddhism. It is necessary for us to consider, as far as is feasible, those themes which Buddhist scholars came to hold as essential to the Buddhism of their time, whether we would consider them present in the earliest discoverable formulations of Buddhism or not.[14]

We have indicated the central significance of the conception of Karma for both Hindu and Buddhist thought. At first glance this appears to be a force or conditioning limitation which has the inevitable result of imposing absolute causality upon all being. In many respects it is of such a character. There is no conception, no impulse, no movement which does not create a new condition of being as an inevitable result. The Buddhist writings are filled with dialectics that seek by logical argument to establish the truth of this understanding of being. To be is to be a resultant of past being, and both past and future being are consequential and contingent.

This first impression of Karma and the Law of Dependent Origination is essentially a correct one, but it does give to the non-easterner a conception of absolute determinism in all things which erects a barrier to a full understanding of the Buddhist view of release from existence, from the law of Karma. What would appear to be, and to a large extent is, a metaphysical presupposition of absolute determinism, arrived at by a consideration of processes and conditions within the empirical sphere, seems by its logic to create an immovable obstacle to the attainment of a state of non-being wherein the limitations of being are removed.

Two elements are important to a more complete understanding of the Buddhist position. First, the total complexity of the doctrine must be comprehended, and, secondly, the Buddhist view toward Time or History must be taken into account. The complexity arises in large part from the total all-inclusiveness of the concept of Dependent Origination, particularly when it is understood that this does not mean an absolute restriction upon the will of the thinking being. All that is results from prior conditions, but they are many and varied in their potency. Each new situation possesses within it the potentiality of variety as a result of the wide range of differing elements which have served to form and structure the new condition. The decision that must be and is made in this new context, is one which is determined within the new and unique unity of past causes in their present effect. All those separate conditioning strands which now unite to create the present, including the similar elements which endow the mind and its contemporary will in its understanding of the present, are not to be understood as producing their separate distinct results. Their effectiveness is a complex; it is a unity composed out of the but momentary individuality which they never in actuality possess. They are in conjunction, in a relationship of identity wherein each is influential upon the other and each is in itself a resultant, at any moment, of the impact of all other elements upon it. Error arises in the understanding of the Law of Dependent Origination when it is based upon a quantitative weighing of all actions and their nature without a corresponding emphasis upon the qualitative weight which they possess. This error is then compounded when it is not remembered that the inertia and potentialities of a past condition may be overcome by the greater inertia and potentialities of another condition. When such a situation or change of form takes place, the inertia of the first condition has had its causal effect in creating a third condition which is the result of the conjunction of the first two states of being.

The first condition has instantaneously ceased to exist by virtue of the relationship it has had with the second condition. Yet it may be said to continue to exist in the effect it had in the creation of the later situation, not in itself, but in the new form which it has influenced though not determined in basic potentiality because of the great qualitative effect of the second more powerful element which it had confronted. The first condition may, then, be said to have produced its fruit, its effect. But, the fruit is not a thing in itself, rather it is a limiting or enriching influence upon the second condition which results in the third state.

The foregoing is by way of indicating that, while all past conditions are held to be in a causal relationship to all present conditions, the past conditions in themselves can only be said to be determinative as a result of their momentary quality, not on the basis of their momentary separate existence as an entity. Each condition is an infinitesimal particle of the total complex flow of all past conditions of being. Properly it may never be said to have possessed an individuality of its own, for it also is a resultant of Dependent Origination. Dependent Origination is itself subject to itself. As a process it creates itself, as do all things. Man, therefore, while a product of his past, is not limited to his past. He possesses a future which, while it will be a product of the total past, will also be a state of being constantly new and filled with potentiality because of the complexity and uniqueness of all new elements which combine to produce it.

Second, though of less importance in the understanding of Karma, is the conception of Time which was a contribution of the Indian ethos to Buddhist thought. For the Buddhist, history possesses meaning as the scene or stage upon which Karma ridden and created man now finds himself. Present history, the time which is experienced now by a living being, does not possess the finality for that being that it does in the metaphysics of the leading religions of the West. It is of primary, but not ultimate, significance in that this particular experience of time is not the single sequence of events that will be experienced. It is the experience of a series of conditions, but the separate experiences are collectively of an infinite duration. Release from them, for the ever new being arising out of each new momentary condition, can only finally and totally be achieved by the working out of Dependent Origination. Release or enlightenment is not limited to the particular sequence of events which constitute the time we know as this life we are now living. Time is unending; it is the process, the chain of separate but related conditions which amalgamate together through the working of Dependent Origination into what appears to be a single sequence possessing absolute meaning for ourselves. The momentary entity I now think to be myself is not, therefore, restricted in hope for release to the present. The hope for release is not absolutely determined by the past and the present; there is an infinite future possessing infinite possibilities for the working out of what now appears to be "my" limitation.

The Law of Dependent Origination is an essential and continuing theme of Buddhist philosophy. In both Theravada and Mahayana it constitutes the central and underlying foundation to the metaphysical conception of the universe and to the understanding of the realm of empirical existence. In the last decades spokesmen for both groups have made much of the degree to which modern western science and psychology support Buddhist thought and writings.[15]

In its acceptance of the doctrine of Karma from its early Indian environment, Buddhist philosophy also embraced other themes which were related to it and which we have discussed in our consideration of Hinduism. Primary among these are the presuppositions concerning Samsāra, the constant flux and impermanence of existence, and metempsychosis or rebirth. Reflection upon the total doctrine of Dependent Origination will reveal that these two understandings of the nature of empirical reality are, in the case of the former, inevitable, and, in the case of the latter, convenient, deductions from the assumption of the original doctrine. For Buddhism and its thought systems they are self-evident presuppositions established by the enlightenment experience of the Buddha and reinforced by the logic of Buddhist thought.

In our discussion of the historical development of Buddhism we referred to the central importance of the belief concerning the nature of the Person of the Buddha. The positions of southern and northern Buddhism in regard to the Person of the Buddha—in Theravada his pre-eminence as an adored supreme Teacher of this age of world history who attained Buddhahood and, in Mahayana, his status as a divine being who with other divine beings has come into infinite history and operated within the total cosmos for the salvation of all sentient beings—have been fundamental to their subsequent development after their initial divergence. While this difference in emphasis was foreshadowed rather early in the growth of the various Buddhist schools of thought and was not unrelated to the religious background and tendencies of the Buddhist laity, it was not until early in the Christian era that the distinct nature and ramification of these divergent views of the Buddha became clear. The popular religion and cultic activity associated with both groups had not completely turned its back upon the popular deities of the Hindu religious ethos. The monastic schools of thought which constituted the Sangha were, however, concerned with matters of proper doctrine, not merely with that which pleased the religious demands of the laity.

The result in southern Buddhism was a growing distinction between the doctrinal and philosophic speculation of the monks and the cultic practices of the majority of the laity. The first served as a system of thought and an environment for the following of the Middle Path to enlightenment on the part of the religiously and philosophically prepared bhikkhu. The cultic practices, and the beliefs associated with them, gave to the non-speculative laity a supporting outlet for their religious needs as individuals and as a community. While it would be incorrect to maintain that there was no relationship between the two, the relationship did not constitute an inherent unity wherein both were essentially dependent upon each other. Intellectual Theravada helped to mold the total culture, while popular religious Theravada contributed to the spiritual insight and intensity necessary for the rigorous discipline of the Sangha to survive as a viable and appealing vocational path within the society.

Northern Buddhism, on the other hand, succeeded in much larger measure in achieving a greater synthesis between the intellectual and the popular aspects of Buddhism. In a very early attempt to delineate the nature of Mahayana as against that of Theravada, Asaṅga in the fourth century listed as the first principal feature of Mahayana its comprehensive nature. This all-embracing characteristic of Mahayana is to be seen, say Mahayana Buddhists, in that it is not limited to one Buddha alone and his teachings. Truth is not confined to the interpretation of the Buddha who taught men in India in the sixth and fifth centuries B.C. When truth is discerned, even when surrounded and often encased in superstition and ignorance, it becomes a part of the Doctrine which has been revealed to mankind in different ages and circumstances of history by various Buddhas.[16]

This Mahayana conception of the incarnation or emergence of Buddhas into the realm of Samsāra, the sphere of mundane and supra-mundane Dependent Origination, gave foundation to a cultic and popular expression of Buddhism which brought the philosophical activity of the scholars and the religious beliefs and practices of the laity into close relationship. While it does not mean that the thought of the intellectual Buddhist monk was shared by the layman, it does mean that the activities and beliefs of each served to complement that of the others. The personal application to the rigors of the Middle Path by the spiritually and intellectually inclined was more closely related to the religious practices and faith of the masses. The former had a place in their philosophy for the variety of Buddhas who were worshiped individually and collectively by the latter. Doctrinal and philosophic presuppositions did not create a wide gulf between the two, wherein the intellectual expressions of Mahayana held the non-intellectual faith of the laity to be essentially unrelated to the Dharma, the Buddhist message to mankind.

Since its beginnings, then, an essential theme of Buddhism has been the Person of the Buddha and his part in the revelation to men of the truth of the human condition. For Theravada his role is pre-eminent though not divine; for Mahayana his role is important, though not unique nor necessarily supreme, but he is divine. From the perspective of religion, the former has no place for a divine being who is worshiped and considered currently active in the affairs of men, while the latter furnishes men with many divine beings worthy of worship primarily because they are active throughout infinite history in bringing men to the enlightenment that is salvation and release from existence.

A doctrine which has been fundamental to all Buddhism, and which constituted one of its primary differences from Hinduism, is the conception of Soullessness (*Anatta*), non-ego or non-self. While the conception of the self (*Ātman*) had early become a primary theme in the development of Hindu philosophy, Buddhism in both of its major forms has denied the validity of the concept and has insisted that all rational evidence supports its denial. Where Hinduism maintains that the mistaken identity of the self with empirical events, with Samsāra, is the ultimate cause of man's predicament, Buddhism declares that a primary cause of man's attachment to existence is his erroneous assumption that he is a continuing self. One proclaims the root of mankind's trouble is the confusion of the self with the world; the other asserts that the problem lies in the conviction that there is a self.

The Buddhist emphasis upon Dependent Origination, the absolutely fundamental first Buddhist presupposition, serves as a basis for the philosophical defense of the doctrine of Soullessness. It is from the first theme that the second proceeds. If it is agreed that *all* that is, any entity, event, or thought within the sphere of existence, is the resultant at any given moment of prior entities, events, and thoughts, it then follows that no thing within existence can be said to be permanent. It changes with the instantaneous and immeasurably small passage of each sequence of time. What "I" was an hour ago, "I" am not now because of the experiences and the thoughts which have been "mine" during this past hour. Likewise, what "I" am after the passage of the smallest fraction of time is different than what "I" was before because the present "I" has been subject to the flux inherent in any passage of time. A new "self" has replaced the old "self," and the old cannot be recaptured except by memory which is a function of the present "self" with its present and different conditioning. Given the presupposition that to be, to exist, is to be in a condition of experience and change, of becoming and not being, the foregoing deduction as to the impermanency of the "self" is an inevitable conclusion. The existence of a changing "self," a soul, an ātman is not necessarily denied.

However, Buddhist philosophy does not stop at this point in its argument, content merely to have suggested that the soul or self is of a changing nature. From the earliest days of the teaching of the Doctrine, as recorded in Buddhist literature, the Buddha and subsequent philosophers have constructed arguments seeking to prove that there is no ultimate essence within, or related to, individual entities such as man. What is it that constitutes a thing, that gives us the ability to refer to it in contradistinction to another thing? It is only the observable measurable characteristics discerned in the thing to which we are referring. By use of objects, such as the chariot, for illustration, Buddhist thinkers seek to establish that no separate item within the total chariot may properly be said to be the chariot. Subtract one item and you do not have the chariot. Subtract all separate parts, or any combination of them, and the remainder does not constitute a chariot. There is no entity to be found which may properly be termed the chariot to which you first referred if any item inherent in it as it first was is subtracted from it, or if anything new has been added to it. Any thing to which a name is given is only the particular unity of separate things in a discernible relationship with each other at the precise moment the appellation is first given. There is no actual or real category of chariot, no chariotness that is permanently inherent to certain things and absent from other things. Names and terms we apply to entities are only convenient means used to denote a temporary relationship that we are able to identify in contradistinction to other complexes of relationship. We know that these relationships are not permanent, that they do undergo change, and that with the dissolution of the relationship the prior name is not now properly applicable.[17]

If the foregoing reasoning is applied to the phenomenon we term a particular individual man, we arrive at the same conclusion. In Buddhist philosophy it is thus demonstrable that such an individual is only the momentary relational unity between separate entities or aggregates (*Skandhas*), impermanent in themselves and their relationship, with no entity that can properly be identified in a real or permanent sense as a continuing element or essence to the relationship. The existence of a permanent "self," "soul," or "I" is argued to be contrary to all logic and demonstrable fact. It was proclaimed by the Buddha to be a false assumption which misleads men. The individuality of a related sequence of changing entities, subjected collectively to a series of changing events, has erroneously been considered to be a continuing entity itself which survives, in essence, the alterations inherent in the experience of movement. Any process is related, but has been mistakenly assumed to be related because of an essence which maintains its identity within the process, whereas the only connection lies in the related nature of the process itself.

Buddhist philosophy has maintained the theme or doctrine of No-Soul as fundamental to the Buddhist understanding of man and the universe. For Theravada such an anthropology has served as logical support for its contention that there is no self or soul which survives after the cessation of this life. There is only the Karma, the impulses toward future conditions in existence, the necessary states of being which are the result of Dependent Origination. For Mahayana the same is generally true though, as we shall discover, there is an element within each existent unity that is inherently related to an Element beyond the limitations of Samsāra and Karma.

Before turning our attention to the theme of Nirvana, it is necessary that we consider the attitude of both branches of Buddhism toward the Divine. It will be evident from our previous discussion that Theravada, in its intellectual form, has no place for a belief in the Divine in the sense of an Ultimate Unified Absolute. Allowing, or assuming, the existence within the universe of beings of a different order from the creatures which populate the earth, Theravada has not declared in any strong fashion that gods do not exist. The Pali scriptures quote the Buddha speaking of gods, and the early disciples making reference to them. These "divine" beings are believed to have different, and often greater, powers than men; they are not considered necessarily further on the path to enlightenment than men. In fact, for the gods to attain release from their particular forms of existence, would appear to be more difficult than for men to achieve the release which the Buddha reveals to them. Gods, then, are to be understood in Theravada thought as beings who are limited to their own form of existence and are not to be equated in any way with the Divine as an Absolute God or Unity creating and governing all existence. There is no God, no Creator, no Absolute. There is only the Law of Dependent Origination which operates as a process.

Mahayana Buddhist philosophy and religious practice are very different in this matter. It is this difference, in regard to what in western terminology is usually referred to as the Divine, that makes it most difficult, and perhaps improper, for students of religion and philosophy to discuss Theravada and Mahayana together as if they were but slightly different variations of the same basic philosophical-theological system. Theravada as a philosophy, as system of thought and ethics, does not fit the classical definitions of religion which in one form or other include the concept of God or the Divine. To the degree that it does have a place for gods or divine beings in its popular cultic manifestations, it is a polytheistic religion. Such belief and practice aid the laity in the comprehension of the working of the universe; they are of no real import to the bhikkhu who has set out on the Path to enlightenment.

In the development of Mahayana certain philosophical concerns and avenues of speculation led to the establishment of a doctrine of an Ultimate Absolute not unlike the Brahman of classical Hinduism. Since the great outburst of intellectual activity which marked the early centuries of the Christian era, a central theme in Mahayana schools of thought, serving to distinguish and separate Mahayana from Theravada, has been the existence of the Divine (*Dharmakāya*). This Divine is the Absolute, the Ultimate of the myriads of universes, realms, spheres, and dimensions which constitute all existence and non-existence. The first thing to be noted about the Divine is that, in its ultimate aspect, like the Brahman of Hinduism, no positive predicates can be made concerning it. Beyond all human comprehension, all measurement, all limitations of being or potentiality, it is not to be established by reason which is limited to perceptions within the limitations of existence. And, while Buddhist and other scholars will rightly object that there are differences in the Mahayana understanding of the Dharmakāya, for our purposes it will be helpful to suggest that much of our previous discussion of the Brahman of Hindu philosophy is applicable to the Absolute of Mahayana Buddhism.

It is the Dharmakāya which fulfills the function of a philosophical Absolute in Mahayana philosophy and serves as the divine Godhead for Mahayana religious speculation. The divine beings present in Mahayana thought, unlike the divine beings we noted as highly limited creatures in Theravada, are manifestations of the Dharmakāya. All beings, at any level or stage of existence or non-existence, are related to the Dharmakāya which is dormant within them at the lower levels of being and progressively more awakened in them at the higher stages of being. It is the Dharmakāya, the Absolute, which is the ultimate "state" behind all states of being comprehensible to existent beings. Because it is a "wholly other," separated from all states of being, it may be said to be in the realm of non-being. But even this statement is only by way of momentary suggestion or inference. The Dharmakāya is not to be limited to non-being if that at all infers absolute removal or isolation from the sphere of being.

It is upon the philosophical ground of the conception of the Dharmakāya that Mahayana Buddhism erects the theology in which it gives place to the divine stature of the earthly Buddha and the numerous Buddha-beings constituting the objects of worship and the sources of revelationary truth for the Mahayana monk and layman. It gives the foundation for the existence of other Buddhas in other ages of history and places the Buddha of India in a context which both elevates him above his fellow men to the status of a divine being and yet denies him uniqueness or even priority within the hierarchy of Buddha-beings who have operated, do operate, or will operate in the sphere of history. The ascertainment of ultimate truth, the truth which, in its ultimate absolute essence, is identified with the Dharmakāya, but which, in the realm of Samsāra, can only dimly and imperfectly be perceived, is dependent upon the manifold activities of many manifestations of the Ultimate Absolute which are continually involved in the work of aiding all sentient life to progress beyond Samsāra.

Mahayana understands all sentient life, and man in particular, to be in possession of the Dharmakāya. More precisely, this means that every man possesses the Buddha essence, the essential element of the Dharmakāya, actually in embryo and potentially in totality within himself. All beings will in infinite time ultimately attain Buddhahood. They are aided by the revelation which comes through the many sources of truth and compassion which flow from the Dharmakāya. The Dhyānī Buddhas, the Mānuṣī Buddhas, the Bhaiṣajya Buddhas, the Sambhogakāyas, the Nirmāṇakāya, the future Buddhas, the Bodhisattvas or Buddhas to be—all of these and more are manifestations which flow into the varied realms of existence to instruct, to nurture, to enlighten, to save all beings.

It will readily be realized that the difference between Theravada and Mahayana metaphysics concerning the positing of an Ultimate Absolute, as well as the disparity in the stature accorded to supramundane beings, has created a wide divergence between them in philosophical and religious matters. In one case there is no Absolute to give an ultimate ground of being upon which all existence and non-existence is to be founded, in the other there is an Ultimate which serves as a base, though infinitely removed, for the process of being and non-being which constitutes the totality of history and its cyclical movement. In neither case, however, is the absence or presence of an Ultimate Absolute made the reason for the hold of Dependent Origination upon existence or allowed to serve as an entity or agent working in essential contradistinction to it. For Mahayana, the Dharmakāya is not the Ultimate Unity which contains within Itself all process, all being and non-being, actual and potential; yet the Dharmakāya is, in an ineffable manner, the Ultimate which constitutes the infinite goal of all spheres of existence and non-existence.[18]

The foregoing is of primary importance in the differing expressions of the two Buddhist groups in their attempts to delineate the nature of Nirvana. For Theravada, Nibbana is the goal of the Middle Path, and for Mahayana, Nirvana is similarly the *summum bonum,* the supreme good, which is liberation from existence as man knows it. For each of them it is ineffable in its ultimate essence, non-comprehensible to the human intellect for the very reason that it is beyond the conditions and limitations of the intellect.

Theravada thought concerning Nibbana may be said to hold primarily that Nibbana is the extinction of all delusions and limitations which constitute existence. The historic and contemporary Theravada expressions in regard to Nibbana reflect the records of the Pali literature concerning the Buddha's experience of enlightenment and his teachings to his disciples both as to the means of attaining the experience and the impossibility of expressing its ultimate nature, content, or lack of it.

Since it is a condition or non-condition wherein there is the complete cessation of all those factors and experiences associated with the realm of being and its process, Nibbana is to be understood as a dimension in which such process and conditioning limitation is absent. Existence is identical with change; Nibbana is non-existence

since it is beyond change. To exist is not to have arrived at a state
or condition in which process is absent, rather the essential nature
of existence is to be a part of process itself. To be is to exist within
a process which involves a becoming of something which is different
from moment to moment. To be is to become, yet it does not mean
that the new state or condition is a final achievement or level which
remains constant and is now removed from the very process which
has brought it into being. Nibbana is thus an end of becoming, for
it does not involve or contain within it process which is but another
term for becoming. It is not an annihilation of the self since there
is no self to be annihilated. It is not the destruction of anything that
is permanent, for in Theravada thought there is nothing permanent
in existence. Rather, Nibbana is a freedom from being, a release
from existence with all the changing, disappearing, and renewing
fetters which constitute existence. It is the cessation of an individual
or related sequence of events and conditions, an extinction of all
past and present causes so that no future effects may occur.

Almost all that we have said in relation to the Theravada position
is equally applicable to the Mahayana understanding of Nirvana.
It is an extinction of the various momentary components (*Skandhas*)
of an individual series or process. They are not only dispersed or
removed from relationship with each other, they are in their separate
parts dissolved. However, the Mahayana presupposition of the
Dharmakāya gives a foundation for an additional conception of
Nirvana which goes far beyond the Theravada view. Mahayana
metaphysics equates absolute or total Nirvana with the Dharmakāya
Itself.[19] Its conviction that the Dharmakāya is present in all individual existences and is the Ultimate Unchanging Absolute unlimited by Dependent Origination, leads Mahayana thought to
maintain that Nirvana is ultimately identifiable with the unchanging ineffable supra-Karma level or dimension of the Dharmakāya.
The nature of total Nirvana, therefore, can be suggested by the conception of the extinction of all factors of Dependent Origination to
the degree that all that is left in any individual process of cause
and effect is the Buddha-nature which is and always has been present. The process and its causes no longer exist; the Buddha-nature
is now Itself without the limitation which has been imposed by the
erroneous assumption of the process, that it, the process, is a per-

manent entity identified with and yet distinct from the sequence of experiences which create it.

Generally speaking Theravada philosophy has held that Nibbana is only to be experienced at the total cessation of the life process.[20] Mahayana has recognized the existence of degrees and types of Nirvana which differ in that varying "depths" of Nirvana are experienced. For example, there is the Nirvana (*Upadhiçeṣa*) that is attainable in life. At this level the Dharmakāya is no longer in a state of rest or dormancy, but the individual is still subject to Dependent Origination that still remains as an effective cause which limits the individual to the process of Samsāra. There is a "residue" which must yet be worked out within the sphere of space and time.[21] There are thus levels of Buddahood, enlightenment, or release from Samsāra. And in each successive one the Buddha-nature, dormant before the Path was begun, is brought into a greater predominance over the fetters, the ties, that have heretofore been binding.

It will be noted, in retrospect, that Theravada and Mahayana Buddhism collectively possess an understanding of man and his existence which maintains that real value—truth—is not to be identified with empirical existence and its limitations. It is important, however, not to make the mistake of concluding that either of them is totally negative in its estimation of the world-process. It is within the experience of existence that men embark on the Middle Path; its methods of procedure are ways which are meaningful within the world, and the compassion for sentient life, a recurring theme of Buddhism, is a deeply felt concern for worldly existence, its limitations and its potentialities.

Buddhism, therefore, is a modern philosophy and religion which presents to the contemporary world themes that continue to attract the attention of mankind. Life as a process of continuing events and conditions with all of its limitations and potentialities, the past that greatly influences the present but which can be overcome, the future as an existence within the world and society, possessing real meaning and significance because of its promise of fulfillment in more rewarding participation in the process, and above all the present as *the* scene of the potential attainment of enlightenment—these continue to make the message of Buddhist thought relevant

to sensitive and thinking men and women. It is the burden of
Buddhist philosophy in the present age of history to seek to express
these Buddhist themes with relevance and clarity.

3

The multiformed expressions of Buddhism today do not lend
themselves easily to an analysis of the present concerns of the religion as a whole. The investigator might have little difficulty in
determining what he thinks should be the concerns; however, he
cannot assume they will be either recognized by Buddhists or necessarily correct from the perspective of the religious faith itself. Also,
in the case of Buddhism, there is the ever present question whether
the breadth of its variety has not resulted in separate religions whose
only common interest is what is inherent in all religions everywhere and, therefore, not something distinctively uniting those
groups classified under the general term Buddhism.

Like all systems of thought and ways of living which bridge successive ages and generations, Buddhism has been required to adjust
to new conditions. Whereas, in the past, this requirement was met
in most instances in a manner which appears leisurely from our
perspective, today such cannot be the case. Contemporary Buddhism
has, therefore, a primary concern in the adjustment of its thought
and social form to the conditions of the last half of the twentieth
century. This it cannot escape, nor do its perceptive leaders desire
to do so. Such leaders are few in view of the great number of adherents to Buddhism, and their scarcity is disturbing when the
traditional place of eminence of the religion in the Asian world
is remembered. Nevertheless, they do exist and their voices are
beginning to be heard.

Professor Wing-tsit Chan has pointed to the long history of the
transformation in Chinese Buddhism from an otherworldly outlook
to a worldly one.[22] Westerners who have fallen into the trap of the
generalization that the western religions are concerned with the
world and the eastern religions are not, have failed to comprehend
the degree to which religions such as Buddhism have both partici-
pated in the worldly lives of their people and emphasized the life
of the spirit, in many instances quite similar to the religions of the

West. The generalization is helpful only when used by the scholar who is precisely aware of the context in which he makes it, and even then it is to be questioned. It is dangerous and erroneous when it is used to differentiate the religions without adequate knowledge of its hazards. In company with Christianity, for example, Buddhism has preached a Gospel which has found much of its popular appeal in its emphasis upon future life. But, unlike most orthodox expressions of Christianity, this religion of the East as a result of its themes has been more retiring from the affairs of the world. This is true, and yet investigation of the history of Buddhism will demonstrate that Buddhism, in the context of the eastern cultures it has been a part of, has played an active role as a participant and as a teacher of a way of earthly life.

In Japan, also, Buddhism has been active in those areas which are associated with the problems of earthly life and the betterment of mankind.[23] The fact that modern political philosophies, events, and governments have supplanted much that has been the responsibility of religions, does not alter the concern of Buddhism for these matters; nor does it remove the need for Buddhism's active participation in the creation and nurture of the proper atmosphere for its activities.

In Southeast Asia much the same is true. In the past these areas have not seen the development of strong centralized governments and economies, with the result that their pace of life has been leisurely, and they have been slow to social ferment. But they have not been totally isolated from the outside influences which have stirred the whole of the eastern world in the past century. Since the Second World War in particular, Theravada Buddhism has found itself united with new societies and nations which are seeking a self-identity in the twentieth century.

In company with the other leading religions of today, Buddhism has a primary concern in the maintenance of itself as an integral part of the society and culture which surrounds it. While such an attempt will rest ultimately upon the philosophical-theological themes we have been discussing, it will be dependent for success upon the application of those themes as support to programs of action in the social and political spheres. Themes, which may appear in final essence to direct men's minds to the supra-mundane, are required to lead men to worthwhile activity within the world. To maintain that they have not done so in the past would be to ignore the history of Buddhism. To conclude that they shall not be able to do so in the future would reveal a failure to understand the themes and their dynamic.

An additional concern of those Buddhist leaders who are aware of the present condition of Buddhism, and the situation it faces in its historical environment, is the need for unity among the various Buddhist groups. The emphasis of Buddhism, especially in its early teaching, upon the solitary role of the individual seeker for Enlightenment, has left a strong tradition which supports individuality and separateness by groups. Despite the refuge which the individual takes in the sangha, and the support which he finds in the total Buddhist social environment, through much of Buddhist history the Path to be followed has been understood to be ultimately his alone. This does not mean that the pressures of environment have no power to guide the individual into the thought and actions of the majority around him. Nor does it mean that agencies outside himself are not operative in his attainment of Enlightenment. It does mean, however, that, as Buddhism spread itself among many local cultures, it underwent a process of fission which constitutes one of its greatest problems in the present day.

The problem of unity within religion has not been as consciously present in Hinduism and Buddhism as it has in the religions of the West. Singleness of doctrine and integrated, cohesive, organizational structure, while not present in any of the religions we are considering, are certainly less in evidence within the eastern religions. For Buddhism, the wide geographic diffusion, accompanied by the confrontation of separate indigenous cultures, has resulted in the development of forms of the religion far removed in content and spirit from the early features and attitude of the original religious experience from which Buddhism sprang.

Today, Buddhism is faced with the question whether its impact upon mankind is weakened by a lack of organizational unity or minimal, purposeful cooperation. Is there a proper and a needed place within contemporary Buddhism, in all of its various branches, for organizational structures and doctrinal discussions that will give the whole of the Buddhist world a consciousness of its unity and its dynamic for meeting the problems of man? Is there strength to be gained from unity, a strength which is not now present but greatly needed? To what degree is it possible for the separate groups within Buddhism, not just Theravada and Mahayana but the divisions within them also, to find common grounds of faith and similar patterns of order which will enable them to rise above their historic differences into a new conception of their inherent oneness? And, most important of all, are such possibilities with their attendant consequences merely the results of western impetus and patterns, or are they indigenous and integral to Buddhism itself?[24]

In the midst of the many problems which are now making themselves evident to the leading religions of the world, Buddhism, as the primary religion of southeastern and eastern Asia, finds itself confronted by challenges which can neither be avoided nor lightly dismissed. It shares the burden of the other great religions in the modern day and, as a result of its own themes and their historical evolvement, has its own peculiar difficulties and potentialities.

NOTES

[1] H. C. Warren, *Buddhism in Translation* (Cambridge: Harvard University Press, 1900). For dependent origination see: the *Sámyutta-Nikáya*, XXII, 90, p. 165 f.; the *Visuddhi-Magga*, XVII, pp. 168 ff.; the "Mahā-Nidāna-Sutta of the *Dīgha-Nikāya*, pp. 202-208.

[2] It should be noted that Buddhist terms are sometimes given in their Pali form and sometimes in the Sanskrit form. Pali, the language of early Buddhism, is to be associated with Hinayana or Theravada Buddhism, while Sanskrit is associated with the Mahayana expression of Buddhism. We shall attempt to use the form most proper to the particular context of our discussion. Hence,

Pali	Sanskrit
Anatta	Anātman
Bhikkhu	Bhikshu
Bodhisatta	Bodhisattva
Dhamma	Dharma
Kamma	Karma
Khandha	Skandha
Nibbana	Nirvana
Tipitaka	Tripitaka

[3] Its influence, of course, has not been limited to Buddhist adherents and scholars alone. For example, T. R. V. Murti raises the question as to the influence of Buddhist Mādhyamika philosophy upon the Advaita system of Shankara. Murti, *The Central Philosophy of Buddhism*, pp. 109-117.

[4] Warren, *Buddhism in Translation*, pp. 392-486. Scriptural discussions of the monastic order.

[5] S. Radhakrishnan (trans.), *The Dhammapada* (London: Oxford University Press, 1950).

[6] W. E. Soothill (trans.), *The Lotus of the Wonderful Law, or the Miao-fa lien-hua ching* (Oxford: The Clarendon Press, 1930).

[7] The Buddhism of Tibet, known as Lamaism or Tantric Buddhism, is generally classified as Mahayanist. However, as a mixture of Hindu mysticism and cultus, pre-Buddhist Bön religion, Mahayana, etc., it is more properly a separate type of Buddhism. See:

Charles Bell, *The Religion of Tibet* (London: Oxford University Press, 1931).

W. Y. Evans-Wentz (trans.), *The Tibetan Book of the Dead* (London: Oxford University Press, 1927).

——, *Tibetan Yoga and Secret Doctrines* (London: Oxford University Press, 1935).

L. A. Waddell, *The Buddhism of Tibet* (2nd ed.; Cambridge: W. Heffer and Sons, Ltd., 1939).

[8] Warren, *Buddhism in Translation*, pp. 129 ff.

[9] PeMaung Tin (trans.), *The Path of Purity, being a Translation of Buddhaghosa's Visudhimagga*, Pali Text Society Translation Series (London: Oxford University Press), Vol. I, 1922; Vol. II, 1928, 1929; Vol. III, 1931.

[10] E. H. Johnston (trans.), *The Buddhacarita or Acts of the Buddha*, Part II, (Calcutta: Punjab University Oriental Publications, No. xxxii, 1936).

F. Weller, *Das Leben des Budda von Açvaghosa* (Leipzig, E. Pfeffer, 1926).

[11] T. R. V. Murti, *op. cit.*

Radhakrishnan, *Indian Philosophy*, vol. I, pp. 643-669.

[12] S. Levi (trans.), *Mahāyāna sūtrālamkāra, expose de la doctrine du Grand Vehicule selon le système Yogācāra*, Bibl. Hautes Études (Paris: H. Champion, 1907-1911).

[13] L. de La Vallee-Poussin (trans.), *L'abhidharmakośa de Vasubandhu* (6 vols.; Paris: Paul Geuthner, Louvain, J. B. Istas, 1923-1926).

[14] That Theravada today is representative of the earliest form of Buddhism is not as easily established as some southern Buddhists would claim. Also, the degree to which the various forms of Mahayana have departed from, enlarged upon, or ignored what would appear to be the earliest Indian Buddhism is a problem of importance to the scholar in understanding Buddhist history and thought.

[15] R. H. L. Slater, "Modern Trends In Theravada Buddhism," *Modern Trends in World Religions*, ed. by J. M. Kitagawa (La Salle, Illinois, The Open Court Publishing Company, 1959), p. 249 f.

[16] D. T. Suzuki, *Outlines of Mahayana Buddhism* (London: Luzac, 1907), p. 62 f.

[17] Warren, *Buddhism in Translation, The Milinda-pañha*, 25.1, pp. 129 ff.

[18] Given the wide variety of thought and expression in Mahayana, any such statement concerning the Dharmakāya is open to scholarly criticism. In those instances where the Dharmakāya is conceived primarily as one of the three bodies or aspects (Trikāya) of the Buddha, it is understood more properly as the state of realization of identity with the Absolute by the Buddha. Cf., Murti, *The Central Philosophy of Buddhism*, pp. 284 ff. In other Mahayana expressions the Dharmakāya is held to be the religious aspect or conception of the essence of existence, the Bhūtatathatā. Cf., Radhakrishnan, *Indian Philosophy*, I, pp. 292 ff. The point is, however, that being or process in the empirical sphere is

not the result of a deliberate design of the Absolute which makes It the arbiter of the mundane world.

[19] Suzuki, *op. cit.,* p. 342.

[20] Exceptions to this are noted by Slater, in *Modern Trends in World Religions,* p. 256.

[21] Suzuki, *op. cit.,* p. 344.

[22] Wing-tsit Chan, *Religious Trends In Modern China* (New York: Columbia University Press, 1953), pp. 86 ff.

[23] Y. Y. Tsu, "Buddhism and Modern Social-Economic Problems," *Modern Trends in World-Religions,* ed. by A. Eustace Haydon (Chicago: University of Chicago Press, 1934).

[24] The fact of Theravada Buddhism's aloofness from other religions, even from Mahayana, is of primary importance to the problem of Buddhist unity. See: Slater, in *Modern Trends in World Religions,* p. 224 f.

V

The
Revelation
of Islam

The beginnings of Muslim thought have their source in the dramatic religious experience of the Prophet Muhammad and, even more basically, in the revelation—the Qur'an—which was the center and essence of the experience. Despite the other important influences, both early and late, to which we must direct our attention, these two initial factors are of such overriding significance in Muslim theology that all else must be understood to be secondary. As we have noted in our consideration of other religions, the development of a system of religious thought is a process initiated from a series of religious experiences and insights, a process which maintains a unity because of its continuing consciousness of the initial and unique insight from which it originates. Each religion conceives its own unique beginning to have been preceded by other religious revelation and experience of preparatory value to the great religious insight upon which it depends. For Islam the series of divine revelations and the human experiences of them which preceded the giving of the Qur'an to mankind are important; however, they fade into relative insignificance before the tremendous event which gave birth to Islam itself.

Islam finds in the Qur'an its source, thought, structure, inspiration, and hope. To a degree which is probably unique among the major religions of the contemporary world, Islam is strengthened by this attachment to a literature which is beyond question in its ultimate authority and divine origin. If it is a source of strength for systems of thought in the modern world to possess an absolute literary authority upon which to depend, Islam, equipped with the Qur'an, has that strength as no other religion. It is to this authority that orthodox Muslim thought has always sought, is seeking, and will seek to be true.

Strengthened by the Arabic background of custom and belief which surrounded the religious experience of the Prophet, by the Semitic religious ethos common to the peoples of Arabia and adjacent areas, and by the dynamic of the revelationary event which bestowed the supreme historical insight of God upon man, Islam was prepared to march victoriously through large areas of the West and Middle East. Within a short time after its inception, Islam was brought into confrontation with systems of philosophical and theological thought far advanced in comparison to the Arabic background and Muslim belief which typified its earliest thought. The initial dynamic, both religious and cultural, which enabled Islam to advance far beyond its homeland, was a force which in its earliest phases had little need of the support of intellectual systematization and speculation. In a few decades, however, that religious zeal and military dynamic had created the need and opportunity for Islamic theological thought to come to grips with traditions of intellectual activity far surpassing anything within its own brief past.

This has meant that Muslim theology, in its most productive periods, has existed in a tension between the divine revelation and human religious experience which gave it birth and the religious, intellectual, and cultural expressions which have arisen outside the Muslim religious and intellectual experience. The tension itself has been most consciously felt when the Islamic world has been vividly aware of the universal character of the message of the Prophet and the strength of the resources which that message furnishes for the divine assignment given to all Muslims. Islam has been most actively aware of the universal character of its message at the very moments it has been face to face with the variety of human religious experience and thought. Its periods of intellectual lethargy and unproductiveness have often been those when Islam was moribund as a result of its isolation or the loss of its inherent vivid consciousness of the universal character of the revelation, the Qur'an, and the Muslim responsibility to present that revelation to all mankind.

Tension between Islamic theological thought and its religious and philosophical rivals has often resulted from the Muslim respect for the attainments of the human intellect, while at the same time Islam claims to possess a revelation which supersedes that human attainment. Non-Islamic peoples have often misunderstood Muslim theological thought and belief because of a failure to appreciate the Muslim respect for the human mind and its attainments. Deeply aware of the unequaled place of authority given to the Qur'an, they have assumed this to mean a total depreciation of intellectual thought and speculation upon the meaning and ramifications of the revelation itself. The result has been that the people of the West have not realized the great intellectual attainments of the thinkers of Islam, nor have they given sufficient consideration to the Muslim intellectual insights which may possess value for all men.

The tension between Islamic thought and its neighbors is not unlike the strain which is inherent in Islam itself. It is produced by the juxtaposition of that which is Divine, and therefore superior, with the obviously inferior quality of that which is human. Given the Muslim conception of God and of man, it follows that what is produced by the mind of man cannot be considered, ultimately, of absolute significance. However, it is obvious that man cannot cease thinking and structuring his thought. Despite the absolute and supreme nature of the divine revelation—in fact, because of it— man is impelled to use his reason in order to comprehend the revelation and to discern its import for himself and his fellows. The anxiety produced by this responsibility in the midst, and under the supremacy, of the divine disclosure has created a tension which has produced a humility, coupled with an urgency, that has become characteristic of Muslim intellectual endeavor in its most productive periods. The humility has reflected the deep awareness of Muslim thinkers of their inadequacy in the light of God's revelation; the urgency has arisen out of their consciousness of the demands which that divine revelation places upon them.

Nevertheless, Muslim theologians have also understood that truth is both possible and probable if arrived at through full use of the intellectual powers bestowed upon man by his Creator. Truth cannot be different from the ultimate truth which constitutes the Qur'an. If it is, it is not truth but the result of the activity of men who have not grasped the fullness of God's revelation nor used the full resources of the intellect He has given them. What then does this mean for the claims to truth present in the systems of theological and philosophical thought outside the Muslim community of believers? Again, this truth is seen as having been arrived at through the wrong use of reason in the light of man's endowment of intellectual capacity and in his knowledge of God and His creation. For the non-Muslim this knowledge of God is highly limited and possibly absent altogether; for the Muslim the supreme revelation makes the knowledge available as far as it is ever available to men. The non-Muslim, therefore, operates under a handicap which is ultimate in nature, to be overcome only when he, too, is brought into the full human knowledge of God through the Qur'an and its revelation.

The foregoing appears to us to be of primary significance because it has frequently served as a basis for Muslim appreciation of non-Muslim thought in the history of the development of Islam. Those outside the Muslim religious faith and its associated culture can no longer afford to dismiss the intellectual attainments of Islam on the mistaken assumptions that Islam has not been intellectually productive and has not possessed a great appreciation for intellectual activity wherever it has arisen. People of the West have not comprehended the intense intellectual ferment which has typified Islam in certain periods of its history. And today, because of an obvious lethargy in some areas and aspects of Islam, they all too frequently remain oblivious to the religious and intellectual resources still present within it. Knowing little more than the barest outlines of Islamic history and Muslim theological thought, much of the world outside Islam is suddenly being brought face to face with a powerful religion and culture which is unknown to it.

A discussion of Muslim theology is required to keep ever in mind the primacy of the Qur'an as the revelation of God. Muslim theological thought and speculation, however, is not totally limited to this one divine revelation. If the nature of God is understood in the depth presented by the Qur'an and attested to by the richness of Muslim religious experience, then the human mind is seen as a vital partner in the expression of the revelation. The Qur'an is *the* revelation, to be sure, but revelation does not exist in a vacuum. It requires a human response, not to establish its truth, but to make its truth relevant for human understanding of life.

1

Muslim theology and its development must be understood in the light of the pre-Islamic religious beliefs of Arabia as well as in reference to the Qur'an. In company with the other religions we have been considering, Islam was both a child of the tradition of its religious-cultural environment and an advance beyond it. The preceding religious tradition provided a basis for the human perception of the Qur'an and the revelation which it constituted; it formed a bridge between the message of the Prophet and the culture of his time. For the Muslim *the* revelation of God is the Qur'an; nevertheless, the important role played by the recognized revelation of God prior to Muhammad's reception of the Qur'an is not to be discounted. For the Muslim it recedes into relative insignificance because of the absolute primary and final stature of the Qur'an; yet, through the Qur'an, it is given authenticity as being valuable to those of mankind who have experienced it.

The religious beliefs antecedent to the early Muslims must be classified as being both Arabic and Semitic. They were Arabic in that they were the product of the relatively primitive tribal culture typical of the peoples of central Arabia; they were Semitic in that they reflected, in their broader orientation, the more universal insights of the religious experience of higher cultures in the Semitic world. The former gave to early Islam a concrete relevance to the life of its people, while the latter served as a means for the attainment of a relevance far beyond the limited tribal Arabic world. Together they united in providing Islam with a religious heritage rich in sensitivity to the existence of the Divine and Its relation to man and human society.

The primitive religious consciousness typical of Arabian belief and practice is one which bestows upon its adherents a vivid awareness of the presence of non-human or divine powers. These powers, benevolent or malevolent, are believed to be much like man in their character. They react, like man, to threats and entreaties; they desire their own ends, and they are often capricious in their judgments. Also, though they may possess greater power than man in many things, they are not completely superior to other powers, demonic and human, which have the ability in certain situations to thwart their designs. As a result, the pre-Muslim religious consciousness gave the Arab a concrete and keen cognizance of the presence, in man's environment, of non-human forces with which man must come to terms. The fact that such forces were disparate and not absolutely superior to man in all matters should not mislead us to depreciate the religious intensity and potential spiritual insight and growth of a people with such beliefs. On the contrary, though beliefs of this level may appear to be primitive in comparison with more sophisticated and intellectual religious systems, we fail to comprehend their strength and significance if we overlook the dynamic dimension of the divine consciousness which is present within them. It is this vivid awareness which is most often the fertile seedbed for the development of a full commitment by men to the Divine. The Divine is adumbrated in the many manifestations of power which man, in his relative simplicity of mind, attributes to scattered semi-divine forces, sometimes superior, sometimes little more than equal to himself. Yet, it is in the apprehension of these godlings and demons that the way is often prepared for the knowledge of the Divine which is the property of the more highly developed and intellectually articulated religions of mankind.

The contributions of alien but adjacent religious thought to the pre-Muslim religion of Arabia is a matter of considerable interest to scholars of Islam and its beginnings. Jewish and Christian belief, in broad outline, was known by those Arabs who had contact with peoples of these religions through the normal avenues of military, commercial, and cultural relationships. In some instances people of these religions lived among the Arabs and radiated a concept of religion which was not completely unnoticed by the more religiously perceptive Arabs. The contact between these and the Arabian religion was seldom direct, with the result that often the thought and influence of the former, because of their subsidiary adjacent position, were misinterpreted in ways that later were to have serious consequences for the relation between Islam, Judaism, and Christianity.[1] To what degree Arabic religious thought contained beliefs which directly reflect the later Zoroastrian doctrines of the Sassanian empire and to what degree it received them secondhand through Judaism and Christianity (Persian-Zoroastrian beliefs having influenced Jewish thought from the period of the Jewish exile of the sixth century B.C.), still remains a matter of some conjecture.[2] In any case, both the popular belief of Arabian religion and the doctrines of later Islam reveal the influence of elements present in these religions long before the rise of Islam. Muslim awareness of this relationship is, of course, demonstrated in the content of the Qur'an and subsequent Muslim theology.[3] For the Muslim this in no way reveals a dependence of Islam upon the other religions; rather it is a demonstration of their historic function as preparatory and, therefore, subsidiary religions to the final supreme revelation of the Qur'an.

It was, therefore, in a highly religious ethos that the Prophet Muhammad preached his message of *the* God, Allah, who is supreme over all existence, all men, and all demons. The strong resistence to the Prophet and his preaching is not indicative of an anti-religious bias on the part of the Arabians who heard him but, rather, reveals their strong attachment to the religious beliefs and customs which had been and were still central to the fabric of Arabian life. This traditional attachment, coupled with the vested religious interests inherent to all religious communities, served as a brief obstacle to the acceptance of the Prophet's message, and was a source of religious curiosity and concern before being ultimately transferred to the new Islam.

The personality, character, and genius of Muhammad has been the subject of Muslim and non-Muslim scholarship, particularly in the recent past.[4] Because of the strong and long enmity between Christianity and Islam, western scholars and religious leaders in the past have traditionally depreciated him as a person, paying particular attention to the moral aspects of his life and teaching which were not in accord with the highest Christian ideals. In taking this position they have revealed their ignorance of the conditions of his time and place as well as demonstrated their own misunderstanding of the nature of Islam. Comparing Muhammad the Prophet to Jesus the Christ, they have made the error of assuming that, from the inner perspective of the two religions and their adherents, the two figures fulfilled the same function and possessed the same status. The error arises from the mistaken Christian assumption that Islam claims for Muhammad a divine status in some manner comparable to that which Christianity accords Jesus.[5] It is important that we understand that orthodox Islam does not make such a claim for Muhammad nor recognize the Christian claim for Jesus.[6] However, Islam does see Muhammad as a chosen man of God and of admirable character.

For our purposes it is important that we appreciate the wide range of the personality and powers of Muhammad, a range which includes political and military sagacity as well as spiritual insight and sensitivity. There can be no question but that he was a natural leader of men who, under the dynamic impetus of his divinely given charge, possessed a charismatic quality of great magnitude. However, the political acumen he demonstrated in his later years at Medina and the loyalty he was able to gain from his early followers are secondary in significance to the intense spiritual life and religious receptivity which were the fundamental qualities of the Prophet. We shall leave to others the task of attempting to disentangle historical fact from legendary tradition, but the very fact of his religious genius is evident from the structure of Islamic thought and society. Whether one, as a Muslim, accepts the belief that the Qur'an is not the product of Muhammad's own thought or, as a non-Muslim, takes the position that the Qur'an is the result of the Prophet's own intense religiosity, it remains obvious that he was a man of acute spiritual insight and sensitivity. In the former case, he was deemed worthy of receiving the divine revelation and conveying it to mankind; in the latter, he would stand as one of the greatest of religious teachers in the history of religion.

Having submitted himself to God and His will, Muhammad devoted his life to the preaching of the message of Islam and the establishment of the religious-social community which was demanded by the divine revelation. By the time of his death in 632 A.D., Muhammad had succeeded in creating a community which united the peoples of the Medina-Mecca area of Arabia around a religious belief which was the foundation for their rapid fusion into a strong religious-political force, which within a few decades spread far beyond the boundaries of Arabia. Islam's vivid consciousness of the Qur'an as the revelation of God and the absolute foundation of Muslim faith, has not meant that the Prophet is inconsequential in Islamic thought or historical development. It is the revelation, which is the Qur'an, that gives Islam its *raison d'etre*, but it is Muhammad, in his role as *the* divinely ordained apostle, who has been chosen to mediate the revelation to men. This new community was thus united around a divine revelation and a human personality caught up in the immediacy of the divine command. Since the days of the Prophet it has found its strength in both of them.

The history of the expansion of Islam within the first centuries following the death of Muhammad is, as we have suggested, the chronicle of a relatively unsophisticated people forced, by their sudden successes and exposure to advanced theological and philosophical thought, into a confrontation with the intellectual riches of much of the western and middle-eastern world. As they advanced into areas with long traditions of intellectual attainment and expression, they were required to take into account methods of rational procedure unlike any they had known before. Because of their absolute conviction that the revelation which spurred them on was the supreme truth of God given to men, the early Muslim theologians could not rest without seeking to make this revelation understandable in human terms, in so far as that is possible. This last qualification is necessary because from its earliest beginnings Muslim thought has been aware that the Source of the Qur'an is such that it is inconceivable that human understanding be made a criterion of its truth. Further, it has been recognized that because of this the Qur'an may not necessarily be completely commensurate with even the best of human intellectual insight. The Qur'an, while not necessarily contrary to reason, must be understood as being beyond reason in its ultimate nature. Rightly understood within the faith which recognizes its true nature, the Qur'an may be a guide to the human intellect; it is never ultimately to be judged by it.

The Qur'an, from which Muslim theology takes its lead, is not a systematic theological treatise or a consecutive enumeration of the doctrines of Islam. Rather, as the record of the revelation of God through the mediation of the angel Gabriel to Muhammad, it is believed to be the Word of God as it was revealed over a period of time. It is a series of utterances by Muhammad in which he is reciting the exact words and phrases as they were given to him. Since these recitations by the Prophet were given at different times, and often were brought forth by the circumstances of the moment, there is a disjunction between the various chapters (*suras*) which is most noticeable to the non-Muslim reader. However, for the Muslim, the Qur'an contains all that is necessary to human knowledge for the proper and full Muslim life under God. True, it has been necessary to construct other sources of guidance—the tradition (*hadith*) traceable to the Prophet, his teachings, actions, and injunctions; the custom or practice (*sunna*) established by hadith; the law (*sharia*) which has the Qur'an and Sunna as its primary sources; the principle of consensus (*ijma*) among the learned religious authorities (*ulama*) upon theological and legal matters—but each of these is to be understood as ultimately derivative from the Qur'an in its content and its authority.

In a manner increasingly similar to the theological development in most of the more advanced religions of history, Muslim theology, in the centuries following the death of Muhammad, split into varying schools of thought, each believed to be the correct interpretation of the absolute truth in the Qur'an.[7] In the earliest period of Muslim theological history the problem for Islamic thinkers was the development of a method of exegesis of the Qur'an which would allow a place for theological expression based upon the Qur'an. Despite the fact that Muslims held the Qur'an to be the final revelation of God to man, it did not follow that the intellectually alert adherent of Islam was satisfied to suspend his intellectual concern and curiosity concerning it and the doctrines it presented to the believer. As a result, Islam has always had theologians and philosophers who have used the Qur'an as their source and foundation in attempts at intellectual systematization and coherence.

In the course of this theological development, among the many important thinkers who contributed to Muslim theology, two are of central consequence in the creation of what has become orthodox Islamic thought. Both combined intense theological concern with personal religious commitment that led them to seek for a synthesis of the values within the varying theological-philosophical positions of Muslim scholars. The first, al-Ash'ari of the ninth century, was deeply conscious of the dangers presented to Muslim orthodoxy by any emphasis upon rational consistency in the doctrines of the faith. Having himself been a rationalist, he was well grounded in philosophical method. The result of his theological endeavors, the Ash'arite theology, was a defense of orthodoxy by the use of some of the methods of reasoning which had set the rationalists against the orthodoxy which the general Muslim community had derived from the early traditional understanding of the Qur'an. While the rationalist emphasis upon logical consistency in the tradition of Greek thought had led to conclusions obviously antithetical to the Qur'an and popular faith of Islam, the work of theologians such as al-Ash'ari served to unite the developing theological speculation of the thinkers with the religion of the Muslim community.[8]

The second seminal thinker within Islam, al-Ghazāli, who died in 1111 A.D., reflects in his life and work an especially intense personal religious concern. By the time of his theological labors, Islam had within its thought and religious life a group of conflicting philosophies and tendencies which might well have brought about a disastrous diffusion of Islam as a unified system of theological themes and a community of religious life. With the wide geographical spread of Islam into varied societies and cultures, the inevitable absorption and integration of elements not present in the original Muslim religious faith, beliefs and practices had already arisen to separate areas of Islam and groups of Muslims from one another. While this is inevitable to some degree in any religion which is large in numbers and in the variety of geographical-cultural areas covered, it obviously presents the devoted theological thinker with the challenge to overcome the diversity in those matters wherein it is bringing about a loss of the essential truth and dynamic of the faith. For al-Ghazāli, the loss of religious sensitivity and concern by the theologians in their eagerness for intellectual systematization, and their emphasis upon theological minutiae to the neglect of the spiritual life, was a perversion of Islam. His native intellectual ability and curiosity, coupled with his personal religious life, led him to the conclusion that theology and philosophy in themselves were not conducive to the depths of religious life present in Islam. He turned to the rapidly developing mysticism (*Sufism*) of Islam, and by his leadership he brought about a combination of Muslim theology and personal religious experience which, in company with the theological tradition of Ash'ari, has served as the core of Muslim theology in subsequent Islamic history.[9]

Our reference to Islamic mysticism and its development into a factor of importance in Muslim religious thought and practice by the time of al-Ghazāli will indicate the degree to which Islam was receptive to religious life not visibly present in its origins and very early history. However, the *Hanif* tradition of pre-Muslim Arabia with its emphasis on meditation upon the Divine, and the place of prayer and receptivity to God in the life of the Prophet, do indicate that even within earliest Islam there was a fertile ground for the development of the mystical religious life. Also, in the course of its contact with other cultures and traditions, Islam was confronted by thought and practice which was highly conducive to religious mysticism. Christian, Jewish, Zoroastrian, neo-platonic, and various local popular religious beliefs—each bequeathed to Islam elements which combined to encourage the development of mysticism as an important factor within the totality of Islam. The result was a religious fervor and receptivity which ran the gamut from the highest of mystical insights and literary expressions to the lowest levels of popular frantic emotional and physical ecstasy. At its highest levels it produced for Islam some of the most sublime of mystical religious literature, while the propagation and reinforcement of the faith by the Sufi orders, or schools and communities, served to give vigor to the whole of the Islamic society. At its lowest levels, in appealing to the inherent religious credulity and superstition of the masses, it tended to debase the purity and admirable simplicity of Islamic religious thought and worship.[10]

Among the many groupings of theological thought and community division which have appeared within Islam, one large faction is of particular importance in the history of the Muslim community and its religious beliefs and practices. Many such divisions have arisen out of theological disagreement, or more often political rivalry, only to disappear or to be reabsorbed into the larger community in the process of time. Each has usually conceived itself to be the true interpreter and protector of the faith in the matter or matters which are under dispute. Some have continued to possess a self-conscious identity within Islam though, in the main, the primary initial cause for their being has lost its vigor.

The separation of the large group known as the Shi‘a from the main body of Muslims had its beginnings in a dispute over succession to the Prophet as the leader of the Muslim community. However, as time went on the Shiʻite movement became the home of political and religious discontent susceptible to the appeal of religious belief in many instances clearly outside of the orthodox tradition. From the perspective of Muslim theological thought, the primary Shiʻite position has been related to the doctrine of the Imām. The Shiʻa political conviction, and, ultimately, its theological belief, was that Ali, the son-in-law of Muhammad and fourth Caliph, was properly the only legitimate inheritor of the leadership of the community. In the succeeding centuries Ali came to be looked upon as a possessor of esoteric knowledge, a knowledge which passed from Ali down to his physical or spiritual heirs. These heirs, or Imāms, were held to be endowed with a "Divine Light" which separated them from mankind and gave them a supernatural character. It is obvious that beliefs of this type are a fertile source for conflicting claims to spiritual knowledge and community leadership. This has meant for Shiʻa Islam a history filled with the appearance of rival factions centered around various claimants to the Imāmate.

The fourteen hundred years of Muslim theological history have witnessed the appearance of numerous thinkers and groups seeking to interpret the revelation of the Qurʼan in terms of their individual understanding of the relevance of that revelation to the Muslim community of their time. It is important to note, however, that there has been relatively little theological debate in Islam over the essential themes of the faith. The disagreement and rivalry has most often been over the application of those themes to Islamic society. Despite the various religious orders, schools of thought, and religious-political factions, Islam has been united to a strikingly high degree around the basic theological themes found in the Qurʼan, traceable through tradition back to the Prophet, and recognized through the centuries by the great majority of the adherents of the faith. This has meant that the most fruitful and informative expressions of Muslim theology have often resulted from the confrontation of Islam with non-Muslim religious and philosophical thought.

The past century or two have produced Muslim thinkers and leaders who have become aware that Islam, once again, is faced with the need to articulate its theological themes with the clarity and vigor it demonstrated in the golden centuries of Islam. They have possessed an incisive awareness of the problems that confront Islam as it, too, has been caught up in the dramatic beginnings of the emerging world culture. Few in number, but deeply cognizant of the weakness of Muslim society in the face of the rising tide of western civilization during the past two hundred years, they have firmly believed that the strength and hope of Islam is to be found in the Qur'an and the essential themes it possesses. They have given contemporary Muslim thinkers an awareness that the assignment which the modern world places upon Muslim theology is imperative both because of the themes themselves and the need of present-day men and society.[11]

2

Religious beliefs may properly be termed essential themes of a religion only when they are inherent to the central teaching of that religion in its early formulation and when they continue to possess that position of importance in the subsequent religious experience and faith as it confronts individual and community life. For Islam the themes of its message were present in its initial impetus and have continued to be the central core of its popular preaching and its theological expression. The Muslim theologian of today finds his source of authority in the same dynamic revelation which furnished authority to his earliest predecessors. Their themes are his, and the degree to which he is a Muslim of his own particular time is always qualified by the more important factor of his participation in the religious experience and certitudes which are the unique possession of those who rightly call themselves Muslim in any period of history.

The foremost theme of Muslim thought, the foundation upon which Islam rests, is the proclamation that *the one* God both exists and acts. The fact of the existence of God is the first and determinative theme of Muslim theology. This is not a matter to be debated, nor is it a simple presumption which may be made as a convenient ground for human understanding of the existence and condition of the world and man's situation within it. There is an Absolute Being, a Supreme Being, who is the foundation of existence in the sense that there is nothing which is not dependent upon that Being for

its being. "To be" is to be the result of a creative act which originates initially with Being Itself.

The foregoing was the first element in the preaching of the
Prophet. Muhammad acted upon the absolute conviction that the
primary fact concerning existence is the Being which is at the beginning of existence, a Being which we shall later note is to be
identified not only with existence in its formation but also in the
whole of its process of evolvement and dissolution. God is, and it
is this fact which is the fundamental reality of the human situation
and the total cosmic condition. There is little evidence, if any, that
for Muhammad the certitude of the existence of God was the result
of previous doubt and speculation or even religious meditation as
such. True, he had been a seeker after God. He was one among
others in the pagan Arabia of his time who sought to know the God
who even then was believed by some to be ultimate.[12] But for
Muhammad the reality of *the* God—as a result of his personal experience of God in the dimension of his own life—was established
as a certainty, was the fundamental absolute of his message, the
wellspring of all other themes central to Islam. The God exists, and
the existence of God is established in human consciousness by the
action of God. Man does not, by his own speculation, meditation, or
sensitivity to the truth of his environment and its nature, arrive at
the fact of God.

It is as a result of this two-fold aspect of God—existence and activity—that Islam came into being as a religion resting upon themes
which have continued to be meaningful to men in varying times and
circumstances. God exists, and the fact of this existence is of primary
importance to mankind because God acts. The existence of God is
established by His actions, and His actions follow from the actuality
of His existence. From the perspective of the developed theological
expressions of Islam, neither of the foregoing are necessary predicates to God. Neither serves to limit God, nor to indicate His
totality. But, from the perspective of the believer, the individual
who is confronted by the existence of God as a result of His actions,
the two are one and serve as the source of religious experience and
its resulting knowledge. Muhammad, then, was a Prophet who spoke
as the result of just such confrontation. God was the Source of his
own religious experience, and God was the Source of the themes

which he, a human prophet, had been divinely ordained to proclaim.

From the time of the Prophet Islam has found its *raison d'etre* in the existence of the One God Who, in His act of Self-revelation to man through Muhammad, established both His Being and His relationship to the dimension of existence which constitutes man and his environment. As the famous Throne verse of the Qur'an puts it:

> God
>   there is no god but He, the
>   Living, the Everlasting.
> Slumber seizes Him not, neither sleep;
>   to Him belongs
> all that is in the heavens and the earth.
> Who is there that shall intercede with Him
>   save by His leave?
> He knows what lies before them
>   and what is after them,
> and they comprehend not anything of His knowledge
>   save such as He wills.
> His Throne comprises the heavens and earth;
> the preserving of them oppresses Him not;
> He is the All-high, the All-glorious.[13]

God is the only ultimate ground of being; He is the One Being, and from Him all subsequent being derives its nature and its destiny. However, the Being of God, and the being which is the character of the existent universe, is not to be understood as a matter of relationship or derivation wherein the qualities of the one may be considered to reside in the other. ". . . To Him belongs all that is in the heavens and the earth." Ultimate Being is the creator and owner of empirical being, but neither creation nor ownership implies identity of structure or nature. Empirical being derives its existence and its nature from God in the sense that it is brought into being by Him. Its character is His creation, but it is not a replica of God "the All-high, the All-glorious."

Thus, from the time of its inception, Islam has had as its central and recurring theme the proclamation that One God exists above all else within known and unknown existence. This was the foundation of Islam at its beginnings; it continues to be the foundation of Islam in the twentieth century. There can be no doubt that it shall be the primary theme from which Islam shall proceed in its venture into the emerging world culture which now confronts it.

However, the dynamic which early characterized Islam, and the source of the immediacy of its claims to attention from mankind, is to be found primarily in the one great and decisive event of God's revelation through the apostleship of Muhammad. It was this act, not of man but of God, which brought into the dimension of human life and society the claims of the Divine upon man. For Islam, it was this event which gave ultimate meaning to history, as man must now understand history. Previously the nature of man and his history was the same as it was now revealed to be. The difference after the revelatory event arises not because of a change of ultimate or basic condition; the distinction between the pre- and post-revelationary time lies in the fact that man has now been confronted by the supreme and final knowledge of God which shall be known in the dimension of Time.

It is from the event in which Islam found its being that the second essential theme of Muslim theology emerges. Islam does not rest solely upon the affirmation that "there is no God but God." It proceeds immediately to the confirming assertion "and Muhammad is His Apostle." While we must beware the danger of erroneously ascribing a divine status to Muhammad, nevertheless, it is necessary that we be aware of the unique nature of his apostleship. He is not to be understood as just one in a line of apostles, or revealers, of the Divine to men. There have been others, but individually and collectively they recede into the background when compared to the human being who was chosen by God as the vehicle for the supreme disclosure of Himself.

It is in the two-fold assertion "there is no God but God and Muhammad is His Apostle" that Muhammad is given his place as the supreme human figure in the drama of divine revelation which has taken place throughout history. Because of this position of pre-eminence accorded Muhammad, Islam has been unswerving in its allegiance to him and the divine themes he was chosen to proclaim. The authority of the Apostle of God is derived from God;

the knowledge of that authority is received by men through the prophetic activity of *the* Prophet selected to serve in the "final" and "full" revelation of the Divine.

The dynamic of Islam as a religious community, and the strength of Muslim theology, are each founded upon these two fundamental essentials of Muslim faith. It is because the one God has revealed Himself through the human agency of a man and a community, that that man and that community have understood themselves to be under the divine injunction to religious action within the total community of mankind. An assignment divine in its origin and its intent was received by Muhammad, and, through him, was passed on to the community of believers who submitted to it. They, the society of believers, were called by him to accept the responsibility to conduct their lives in accordance with the revelation and its teachings. And they were also commanded to bring to all men the human knowledge of the Divine and His commands.

The Muslim theme concerning man and the human situation derives from the theme in the Qur'an revealing the nature of God, as well as it contributes to the human understanding of the Absolute God and His Self-disclosure. It is the contention of Muslim theology that man, the creature, must never be confused with the Source of his existence, the Absolute Creator. All men are by nature derivative from God; this is man's essential characteristic. Derivation, however, must not be allowed to suggest likeness. Above all, it must not be confused with an identity of essence which leads man to assert a freedom, thereby contradicting his ultimate status as creature.

Man, therefore, is a creature who receives his existence, nature, and destiny from God. Human denial or forgetfulness of this situation is the sin which creates the real dilemma of the human condition both for individual man and for men in community. The human error is the refusal to acknowledge this dependency and it is compounded by man's confusion of other and false elements with the Ultimate, the Absolute God revealed finally and fully in the apostleship of Muhammad. In company with theologians of the other great Semitic religions, Judaism and Christianity, Muslim theologians contend that the human error is the assumption that the

Divine is discoverable by man and is conditioned or limited in that
It is not in Its ultimacy beyond the categories of human understanding.

Man's situation then, both individually and corporately, is the result of his divine creation confused by the limitations inherent to
his humanity. He himself is not divine nor is he to be considered
related to the Divine by the nature of his origin, so that he partakes
in the Divine nature derivatively by a process of transference or
adoption. Lacking within himself such a stature, he seeks, in his
weakness, to create a situation wherein life is tolerable within the
dimension of his environment. This he does by acknowledgment
and worship of false deities in the mistaken conviction that they
will bring to him a security which he deeply desires and obviously
lacks. Where there has been no real knowledge of God because of
the absence of revelation, this human condition has resulted in the
polytheism and crass superstition Islam attacked in pre-Muslim
Arabia and discovered in heathenism as it spread throughout the
world. Where there has been a knowledge of *the* God, as a result of
the pre-Muslim revelationary activity of God, man has been unable
and unwilling to abandon his commitment to the deities of his own
creation. This he has done not by a total rejection of the God revealed to him, but by a perversion of Him in order to maintain the
independence contrary to the nature of God and the constitution
of man. The preparatory revelations, the earlier Self-disclosures,
while of great value, have not brought men to the human understanding necessary to overcome their limitations so as to fully pre-
pare them to submit to the One God.

Not only have individual men been guilty of the human error,
but men, collectively, in the formation and structuring of their societies have created the means of supporting and perpetuating it.
The early Islamic teachings recognized the relationship, perhaps
identity, of private and public religious, moral, and social belief
and practice, as subsequent Muslim theology has continued to do.
The condition of man is personal and corporate, and where the one
is not a reflection of the other, where a harmony does not exist between the two, neither is adequate in bringing man to the proper
recognition of himself and his plight. It is for this reason that pagan

and erroneous religious cultures and societies reflect error not only in religious belief but also in their community life. Such societies are reflections of an understanding of man which leads to disharmony. Men are caught up in loyalties which are conflicting because they are based upon false presuppositions. Most disastrous of all, human society becomes the support of the weakness of the individual, a weakness which leads to a forgetting of God.

For Islam the structure of human society is of vital importance. In the light of Muslim theological themes, it is readily apparent that all that is must be understood as being under the sovereignty of God. And the community of men is primary in its role of furnishing support to the life that is submitted to the Divine. It is for this reason that it was inconceivable to early Islam that there should be division between religion and state. The truth made manifest in the Qur'an is a truth which cannot be isolated from the important area of intra-personal relationship in the human sphere. It is in this realm as well as in the sphere of the private individual and his relationship to God that the themes of that truth are to operate. In fact, the very nature of the individual submission to the Divine is such that once made it cannot be limited to the individual. It must, by nature, spread out into the arena in which the person expresses his individuality and thereby comes into community with other persons. It is only when the conditions within the community are shaped by the essential themes of the faith that both the individual and the community may properly be said to be living in submission to God and His will.

It follows from the foregoing that Muslim society must be viewed from the perspective of Muslim theology. It is not our task, at the moment, to investigate the degree to which Muslim society has, throughout its history or in any particular period, been in actual conformity to the ideal demanded by the themes of Muslim theology. However, it is essential that we clearly recognize the fundamental Muslim belief that all life is to be lived under God. This has meant for Muslim society that in theory there is nothing which may properly be termed secular. The law which governs men in their daily relationships is, in essence, the same law which is binding upon the individual because of his nature and his submission to God. Therefore, from its inception, an essential theme of Muslim theological thought has been that the only proper structure of society is to be found in a community which itself rests upon, and is shaped by, the full and final revelation which is the Qur'an.

Still another theme of Muslim theology, and an inevitable derivative of the central themes we have discussed, is that of the ultimate and absolute quality of Islam. The absolute nature of Islam, in relation to all other beliefs concerning existence, is to be seen in the ultimacy of the revelation upon which Islam is founded. Islam is supreme in its role as religion and in its place within the lives of men. Those religions which arose out of previous Self-disclosures by the Divine may not be totally in error; they are, however, superseded by Islam to the degree that the absolute and ultimate quality of the revelation of the Qur'an places them in the position of being of little ultimate value. They may be tolerated, but any claims they make for serious consideration by mankind are misleading and, ultimately, false.

Because of the belief that it is the direct result of the supreme act of God in history, Islam, since its beginning, has confronted mankind with a claim absolute and ultimate in nature. It could not do otherwise and retain the integrity of its basic themes. This claim is basic to its theological utterances and to its preaching. It is the source of its dynamic and the support of its certitude. Without it Islam would quickly become the very thing it claims its religious opponents to be—perversions of the truth resulting from the refusal of men to submit themselves fully to God, or beliefs which lack the truth because they are the products of the desires of men without the correction of the divine Self-disclosure.

The primary theme of Muslim theology—the nature of God and His specific Self-disclosure in the event which brought Islam into history—is thus brought into full force in the essential proclamation of the ultimate and absolute quality of the Qur'an. All the recurring themes, which combine to constitute the totality of Muslim theology, rest upon the primary theme and collectively support the final thesis, the Muslim certitude, that together they present the ultimate and absolute truth available to man in history. It is the assignment of Muslim theology in this, as in every age, to express dynamically these fundamental themes to all men.

3

Any discussion of the contemporary concerns of Muslim theology is confronted with the question of whether it is significantly alive to the modern world and its impact upon the essential themes of Islam. Though greatly different from Buddhism in content and history, Islam shares with its Far Eastern contemporary what might properly be termed a theological isolation from the concerns of the present. Politically and culturally caught in the midst of the events and currents which are rapidly changing and conditioning the world as a whole, both of these religions would appear to be as yet theologically and philosophically unaware of the degree to which their themes are in need of contemporary expression.

Adequate consideration of the foregoing question demands that attention be paid to the inner conditions, the essential spirit of the religion, and that investigation not be limited to consideration of the obvious and outward appearances which the religion presents. Theological activity and philosophical concern are most easily discerned through the expressions of the religious-intellectual leadership associated with a religion. However, in any serious attempt to discover the true condition of a religion, even of its intellectual content at any given time, the theological vitality present within the total community of adherents must not be ignored. The intellectual leaders by their leadership serve an important function, possibly a decisive one. They do not, however, constitute the totality of the theological thought and spirit of the religion.

Within Islam in the past century or so, intellectual leaders have arisen who have demonstrated a theological concern founded upon a perception of the contemporary world, its condition, its changing nature, and its challenge to the essential themes of Muslim theology. A cursory glance at them individually, and a general knowledge of their separate careers, easily leads to the conclusion that their impact upon Muslim thought and the world of Islamic society was almost negligible. At least this would appear to be so in the case of those who were cognizant of a need for Islam to confront the emerging culture rather than retreat to the past. The problem for the student of Islam, however, is that of attempting to discover the degree to which their activity was successful in planting within the general Muslim mind an awareness of the present as it confronts Muslim thought and Islamic society. Gigantic as such a task must obviously be, and impossible of final and clear solution because of the imponderables which it confronts, to ignore it would be to disregard the primary source of support for any contemporary theology which possesses meaning in the lives of men and women.

The leading figures of recent Islamic history, especially those associated with the attempt to express Muslim thought in the sphere of theology and society, are relatively few in number in comparison to those which quickly come to mind in a consideration of Christianity or Hinduism. Since the beginning of the nineteenth century the primary names are those of Jamālu-d-Dīn Afghānī whose career led him to activity in various areas of the Islamic world; Muhammad Abduh of Egypt; and, Muhammad Iqbal of India. These men, along with others, have served as the theological-social spokesmen for Islam during the past century and a half as it has been brought face to face with the modern world and the culture which is emerging within it. There have been others who have served more primarily as leaders in the "secular" political and social sphere, and their names are often better known to the peoples of the world, both Muslim and non-Muslim, primarily as a result of their political activities. However, they and their supporters within the Muslim community are the inheritors and beneficiaries of the thought and activity of those who more properly fall within the classification of theologians. But we should not forget that theologians themselves, by their theological activity, may be involved both intellectually and physically in the more mundane world of practical politics and social activity.[14]

The currents of theological-social thought which have been manifest within Islam in the past century or more have demonstrated the presence in the Muslim world of a vitality which many non-Muslim observers in the nineteenth century had failed to perceive. The conservative revivalism of puritanical Wahabism in Arabia itself, the attempt toward the revivification of Islam as a religious and political community by Afghānī, the call to the purification of Islam by Muhammad Abduh, and the plea for a reconstruction of Muslim religious thought by the philosopher-poet Iqbal—these reveal to us a ferment of thought and activity which belies the all too prevalent western conclusion that Islam has lived in the past centuries oblivious to its own condition and the challenge of the surrounding world.

If we remember that Islam is, in a pre-eminent way, a series of theological themes conceived as being inseparable from both individual and community life, we are brought to the realization that as the modern world, in the form of western scientific and political expansion, came into inescapable confrontation with the Muslim world it was incumbent upon Islam to bring its essential themes to bear upon the situation. That in many instances or areas it has been slow in so doing, does not erase the fact that it has done so and is under the absolute obligation to continue to do so. This is not an obligation which arises merely from a theoretical principle; rather, it is a demand which originates within the need of the adherents of Islam as they live their lives in the modern world. The degree to which Islam, or any religion, has been lethargic in meeting this responsibility is a reflection of many and complex factors; it is not to be considered simply as an indication of the inapplicability of the themes or the rejection of them by those who have previously found them meaningful.

The deep-rooted conception of the close relationship and ideal unity of religion and state, inherent in Muslim thought from the beginning, served as a prime source for an awakening to the dangers to Islam present in the political and social conditions of the nineteenth century. The decay of Muslim political strength in many areas, and the rapid advance of European colonialism into the Islamic world could not be ignored completely by the intellectual leadership of the Muslim community. The degree to which it was not an evident concern of the theologians, however, is rather remarkable. The lack of solicitude which did exist may be seen, in part, as a reflection of the internal theological lassitude coupled with the political helplessness and divisions which marked the latter years of the Ottoman Empire. Nevertheless, there were those who were becoming increasingly aware that, as Wilfred Cantwell Smith so forcefully puts it, "something is awry between the religion which God has appointed and the historical development of the world which He controls." [15]

Faced with the evident decline of Islam as a political power in the face of European onslaughts, and cognizant of the lack of internal spiritual dynamic upon which to draw for renewed strength in the meeting of the challenge, men such as those we have previously named set out to strengthen "the religion which God has appointed." Each in his separate way sought, first, to bring about a renewal of the dynamic of Islam in the life of the Muslim peoples. Some maintained that the lack of dynamic was due to the corruption of the Muslim peoples by the invidious invasion of non-Muslim thought and ways of life. These were seen as being contrary to the standards of rigid monotheism and the simplicity of life which was enjoined by the Qur'an. This attempt at revival of what was believed to be the primitive condition of Islam and, therefore, the proper state of life and community, served in the eighteenth century as the rallying cry for the Wahabi movement which continues down until today in Saudi Arabia.

Others, such as Afghānī, placed their emphasis upon the revivification of Islam primarily through political activity which would free the Muslim world from domination by non-Muslim powers. This was to be accomplished by the removal of the endless dissensions, disputes, and divisions within Islam which had destroyed the dynamic of the Muslim peoples and their society. The people were ignorant and helpless, and domestic and foreign governments were either unconcerned with, or opposed to, the strengthening of the religious-social life essential to Islam. The people, and the society of which they were a part, had been corrupted, and now they were unable to meet the needs of their time.

A few, primarily Afghānī's pupil, Muhammad Abduh, devoted their main energies to the revival of Islam by the means of theological activity designed to revive religion intellectually and in the personal lives of the Muslim people. Abduh recognized that while there were many elements in his time which contributed to the lethargic condition of Islam as a religion and as a society, primary among them was the presence, within Muslim belief and practice, of thought and religious activity contrary to the teachings of the Qur'an and the standards set by Muhammad and the early community. While not oblivious to the need to express the essential themes of Islam in forms meaningful to the knowledge of his time (much of his writing and teaching was devoted to that end), he was especially concerned that the inner life of faith in God and His Self-disclosure be strengthened among the people.

All of the seminal thinkers and leaders were theologian-teacher-politicians in the sense that their deep concern with the implementation of the truths of Islam to the conditions of their time demanded that their activities not be limited to one sphere to the total neglect of the others. Those who were noted as theologians primarily drew unto themselves students who were anxious for the strengthening of Islam both as a religion and a society. Those who were active in political intrigue found the basis for that activity in their theological convictions and their personal religious dedication. Each was convinced of the eternal applicability of Islam and its message to the human situation in all times and for all conditions.

The conviction that Islam is dynamically germane to the present, and that this relevance can best be expressed by extended use of the resources of modern thought is seen most clearly in the thought of Muhammad Iqbal. Throughout *The Reconstruction of Religious Thought In Islam*[16] he reveals an awareness of western thought and its role in the development of the present and emerging world. He was prepared to abandon classical Greek philosophy and subsequent speculation dependent upon it. Placing great emphasis upon free and independent inquiry, he sought to reconstruct Muslim theology by an interplay between what he believed to be its own independent tradition and modern "historical" and "scientific" thought. Defensively attempting, whenever possible, to demonstrate Muslim achievements in line with the development of modern scientific knowledge, he also sought to bring the Muslim peoples to a recognition of their own potential role as participators in contemporary and future history. For Iqbal, Islam was the ideal preparation for the present and emerging world. The true spirit of Islam is one which prepares man to participate in life and community under the God who is the creator of History. To be a Muslim is to be prepared for any process of history and any condition of society. By his acceptance of the themes of the Qur'an, the Muslim has been uniquely equipped by God to use the new knowledge furnished to man by nature and history. In the light of *the* revelation which God has given, human knowledge at any period is brought into correct focus and made meaningful for man and society. With such knowledge the themes of Islam are more fully appreciated, and with those themes human knowledge is given the opportunity to contribute to the betterment and salvation of man under the grace of God.

It is on the basis of the thinking and teaching of such theological-social thinkers that those Muslims who are concerned with Islam in relation to the modern world now speak. Deeply influenced by the pioneering attempts of these predecessors, and often knowledgeable of the complex ramifications of the emerging world culture in which they are involved, the contemporary Muslim thinker is seeking to bring to the younger educated generation an awareness of both the Muslim heritage and its application to the world in which such a generation must live. The fact that among the millions of people who are Muslim such thinkers and educated youth are few, is a problem which is not limited to Islam.

Evaluation of the strength and dynamic of a religion for the larger numbers of its adherents, especially a religion which extends over wide areas and includes diverse peoples, is extremely hazardous. For Islam the immediate decades ahead will give some insight into the degree to which the essential spirit of the religion of the Qur'an is vital to the majority of its adherents. In large measure the answer to the question will be determined by whether or not the educated and theologically inclined Muslims of today carry on the assignment given to those who "submit" to the Self-disclosure of God which is the Qur'an.

NOTES

[1] Tor Andrae, *Les Origines De L'Islam et Le Christianisme*, trans. J. Roche (Paris: Librairie D'Amerique Et D'Orient, 1955).

R. Bell, *The Origin of Islam in its Christian Environment* (London: Macmillan & Co., Ltd., 1926).

H. Charles, *Le christianisme des Arabes nomades sur le limes et dans le désert syro-mesopotamien aux alentours de l'hégire* (Paris: E. Lerous, 1936).

[2] For relationships between Islam and Zoroastrianism both before and after the rise of Islam, see: I. Goldziher, "The Influence of Parsism on Islam," trans. by G. K. Nariman in C. P. Tiele, *The Religion of the Iranian Peoples* (Bombay: The Parsi Publishing Company, 1912).

[3] Frequent references are made in the Qur'an to leading figures in the Old Testament, to Jesus, to Mary the mother of Jesus, etc. As examples see Suras III, 1-105, XIX, 16-34.

[4] Syed Ameer Ali, *The Spirit of Islâm* (London: Christophers, 1922). Originally published in 1873 as *A Critical Examination of the Life and Teachings of Mohammed.*

Tor Andrae, *Mohammed: The Man and His Faith,* trans. T. Menzel (London: George Allen & Unwin, Ltd., 1936).

[5] Wilfred C. Smith, *Islam In Modern History* (Princeton: Princeton University Press, 1957), p. 17 f, footnote 13. Contains suggestive comments on this point.

[6] However, note should be taken of the high esteem for Jesus the son of Mary *(Isa ibn Maryam)* throughout the Qur'an. For example, see Suras III, 40; IV, 169; XIX, 21, 31, etc.

[7] The question as to whether Muslim sectarian differences are primarily "theological" in nature or are divisions arising more out of moral-sociological disputes must be kept in mind in any consideration of Muslim theological schools and groups. See Smith, *Islam in Modern History,* p. 20.

[8] *Abu'l-Hasan 'Alī ibn Ismā'īl al-Aš'arī's Al-ibānah 'an uṣūl ad-iyānah* ("The elucidation of Islām's foundation") trans. and notes by W. C. Klein (New Haven: American Oriental Society, 1940).

The Theology of Al-Ash'ari, trans. and intro. by R. J. McCarthy (Beyrouth: Impr. Catholique, 1953).

D. B. Macdonald, *Development of Muslim Jurisprudence and Constitutional Theory* (New York: Charles Scribner's Sons, 1903), Part III, Chap. III, and Appendix I, III.

[9] D. B. Macdonald, "Life of al-Ghazzāli with Special Reference to his Religious Experience and Opinions," *Journal of the American Oriental Society,* XX (1899), pp. 71-132; Macdonald, *Development of Muslim Jurisprudence and Constitutional Theory,* Part III, Chap. IV, and Appendix I, IV.

M. Smith, *Al-Ghazālī, the Mystic* (London: Luzac, 1944).

[10] For Sufism, see:

A. J. Arberry, *Sufism* (London, George Allen & Unwin, Ltd., 1950).

L. Massignon, *Al-Hallaj, Martyr mystique de l'Islam* (2 vols.; Paris: Geuthner, 1922).

R. A. Nicholson, *The Idea of Personality in Sufism* (Cambridge: Cambridge University Press, 1923).

———, *The Mystics of Islam* (London: G. Bell & Sons, Ltd., 1914).

———, *Studies in Islamic Mysticism* (Cambridge: Cambridge University Press, 1921).

M. Smith, *An Early Mystic of Baghdad* (London: Sheldon Press, 1935).

———, *Rabi'a the Mystic* (Cambridge: Cambridge University Press, 1928).

[11] For a discussion of some of these leaders and their part in the shaping of the contemporary Muslim mind and world, see:

C. C. Adams, *Islam and Modernism in Egypt* (London: Oxford University Press, 1933).

H. A. R. Gibb, *Modern Trends In Islam* (Chicago: University of Chicago Press, 1947).

[12] It is important that non-Muslims be aware of the conception of a Supreme Being in pre-Islamic Arabian thought. See footnote 1 of this chapter, and:

K. Cragg, *The Call of The Minaret* (New York: Oxford University Press, 1956), pp. 37 f.

[13] A. J. Arberry, trans., *The Koran Interpreted* (London: George Allen & Unwin, Ltd., 1955), Vol. I, Sura ii, vs. 256. Reprinted by permission.

[14] See footnote 11 of this chapter.

[15] *Op. cit.*, p. 41.

[16] 2nd ed. (London: Oxford University Press, 1934).

VI
Paths
for the
Future

We have sought to demonstrate that Christianity, Hinduism, Buddhism, and Islam have each entered the contemporary world scene with a set of themes inherent in their historic beginnings and developments. No one of them can be separated from these recurring themes without suffering a blow which would finish it and lose for mankind the continuing values which a living religion bestows upon its adherents. That they should abandon these themes in total, or even in part, would be vehemently denied by those associated with each religion, and would be doubted by many who appreciate their past and hope for their future contribution to the spiritual and total welfare of man. We cannot consider the future of religious thought throughout the world without taking into account the past history of these religions and the themes which shaped that history.

It has been noted by many commentators upon the present world scene that the one primarily new condition of human existence is the pre-eminent reality of intra-world relationships. These relationships constitute the present pattern of the fabric of human society, a composite of not two or a few of the traditional societies of the past, but of all groups of mankind. Even those groups which have been classified as pre-literate or primitive are now a part of this unity, a unity which will not allow them to stay isolated nor to retreat to the conditions of their immediate past. Even many fringe societies, obviously destined to be eradicated by the present process, are partners in shaping the process as they combine to participate in it and bring to bear their own interests and peculiar insights. Forcibly brought into this relationship by the powerful societies which have invaded their precincts, at the time this is being written they are at the forefront of the world scene in their claims and in their reactions to the process.

Where it may have been proper in the past to refer to this emerging intra-relationship and basic structure of world society as being the result of *westernization,* today it is becoming apparent that such terminology is both inadequate to the situation and erroneous in its more obvious implications. The world is rapidly becoming a medley, a mixture of forces which are not to be identified exclusively with the West and its modern expressions. This is not to claim that particular features which have been associated with the West in its own development during the past few hundred years and in its expansion and impact into the non-western areas, are not of extreme current importance in the pattern. Rather, it is to call attention to the fact that what the West has contributed is rapidly becoming the property of non-western societies. The pioneering in the initial stages of the development was under western leadership, and the earliest features of the pattern have been western in character. Now the process continues under a leadership which is no longer exclusively western in either background or motivations, and the pattern itself is beginning to foreshadow characteristics that reflect influence and structures which are not western. True, the techniques employed, and often the frames of reference that serve as guides for this new leadership, are still predominantly those associated with the West and its contribution. Yet, in the implementation of the process and the attempts at the construction of a philosophy to support it, it is no longer an exclusive property of the West and its provincial culture. In its present expressions it has become a property of the world and will undoubtedly continue to be so in its future development.

1

The hazardous and presumptuous attempt to chart something of the nature of the religious thought of the future demands that we be well grounded in the past and present of the religions. At the same time we must feel free to strike out into paths which go beyond the past and the present.

Further, the paths to which we turn are themselves not completely new. They will go beyond the past and the immediately present beliefs of religious men and women only in that they will suggest means of reinforcing the old as something of primary worth because it is ever new in its value to succeeding generations. Some of the religions do acknowledge the validity of these paths in the light of their own themes and convictions concerning truth and its revelation to mankind. None of them has not at some time had adherents who have themselves sought to embark on these paths as a result of their own understanding of the themes of their faith.

The first matter we would suggest as essential to the future of religious thought is the necessity that the religions recognize the presence of revelation in all of human history. There is, perhaps, no single item of greater importance to western theology and eastern philosophy than the need to give close attention to the problem of general revelation. We have noted in our discussion of the themes of the four religions that each has at the core of its thought the belief that ultimate truth has been made known to man. Each has its separate understanding of the truth, and each has its own distinct conviction as to how the truth has been made known. The religions are separated from each other, in conflict with each other, partly as a result not of the content of the truth but because of their beliefs that they as individual religions are in a superior fashion the recipients of truth.

They are united in their fundamental conviction that truth is discernible within the sphere of history. Whatever their emphasis upon history, and this is of great importance in their individual constructions of revelation, they conceive the realm of space and time, the area of man's activity, to be one which is not isolated from truth. Truth is in some degree to be known by men. No matter what its ultimate nature, or how far beyond the categories of human intellectual endeavor it may be, truth is not an element totally beyond man and his comprehension or reception. In its ultimate essence truth may be, in fact, according to each of the religions is, so unlike or "other" than anything which can be precisely defined in the human sphere that it is not to be identifiable with human existence in its limitations. Yet truth does invade the human and limited sphere of existence. It is related to it but is not to be identified with it. The significance of history, for each of the religions, is to be found not in the mere sequence of events, in the passage of time that is the structure of history, but rather is to be found in the fact that truth confronts man in the realm of history and its limitations. It is in history that man is brought face to face with truth in its meaning for him now and in the future.

The recognition by each of the contemporary leading religions of the presence of revelation in all of human history, as that history is revealed in the separate chronicles of each of the religions, would not be simply the acknowledgment that truth has not been confined to one stream of history, to one people, or to one moment alone. It would be the verification by the religions of a major theme which is present in them all. It is the assertion that man, despite what limitations or degredation each religion may ascribe to him, is a being of consequence who, by his derivative nature, possesses some potentiality of response to the truth. It would be the proclamation of a recurring theme essential to the messages religions bring to present-day confused mankind—the statement that man is of worth in the sight of the Divine, of value in relation to the truth, despite his present conditioned and restricted existence. It will constitute an affirmation by each of the religions of the religious and intellectual sensitivity of mankind, a sensitivity which each religion has seen revealed among its own adherents in its history and by which it has been enriched in its own particular understanding of the revelation of the truth.

A second path which must be explored further by the contemporary religions is their relationship with the cultures and civilizations with which they have been associated in the past. We have referred in earlier contexts to the importance of these relationships to the religions and their separate development as well as the significance to the cultures which results from the connections. Each of the four religions is identifiable with at least one primary culture and other related or adjacent ones. Because of expansion throughout their histories, they have been brought into meaningful relationship with cultures other than the one which was primary to them in origin and in the major portion of their development. In this new and expanding relationship, these religions have each played a significant role in the subsequent structuring of these "second" cultures. Because of the primary tie between the themes of the religion and the prior culture, the secondary cultures have often absorbed into themselves much of the form, thought, and expression which had become essential characteristics of the first culture. Religion has, therefore, been a dispenser of culture by carrying with it in its migrations the cultures it has experienced during its history. Of course, cultures have themselves fulfilled a similar role by their transmission, as they expanded into new areas, of religious thought and practice that has been a part of their own past. The obvious point to be remembered is that the cultural-religious, or religious-cultural, relationship, while in most cases an interrelation between a primary religion and a primary culture, does not prevent alliances between the religion and other cultures. In past history this second rapport with one or many cultures has been either dominated or highly influenced by the first and primary relationship. In some instances the result has been the partial or total obliteration of the second culture by the religion and the culture most closely related to it.

It is obvious that each of the four religions has a history of primary cultural relationships it cannot deny without rejecting, at least partially, its past and present expressions of the recurring themes which have been considered essential. Each of these religions has embarked upon a course of actions and claims which proclaim its essential themes as pertinent and relevant to mankind within any environment and any conceivable situation. Christianity, Hinduism, Buddhism, Islam—each is now facing the question as to how it can itself rise above the culture which in the past has nourished it in order to make itself significant to men in other cultures while at the same time maintaining a relevant partnership with the first culture. To what degree is it legitimate in the case of each of them to make the separation? Are they so tied to their past cultural environment that, to remove themselves intellectually in their future expressions of thought, would mean the disappearance of their own unique and valuable contributions to human thought? Do they possess within their essential core elements which are properly supra-cultural, and is it possible for them to express them within a multi-cultural, or pluralistic, context with the dynamic they have proved in the past within their original context? These and similar questions are the inevitable results of the present claim made by the religions which seek to be relevant to all mankind.

None of the four religions would allow that the truth each claims to be expressing is itself essentially limited to human cultural circumstances. Even in the sphere of social and ethical systems, the leading religions are more and more demonstrating their recognition of the propriety of social diversity and, within limits, of diverse ethical behavior. In the latter matter, religious ethicists are primarily concerned with the ethical principles and norms which are derived from the specific religion's experience of truth. In the realm of practical application of these norms to individual social situations, they are highly conscious of the local circumstances and limitations which must be confronted as religious men seek to implement the higher principles in daily life. Religious thinkers are coming to understand the complexities which are inherent to the multiplicity of individuals and societies and, in so doing, they recognize that it is their duty to establish the imperative relevance of the truth to all men before seeking to apply it to the particular situation. In their own understanding of their religion, some are going to great lengths to demonstrate that the essential themes of the religion's theological doctrines are distinct from the historical forms of the religion and even from the religion itself. The truth is recognized to be beyond the institutional and cultural religious expression which has served to represent it within the historical community.

We would suggest that the growing conviction that the religions themselves and their themes are not absolutely tied to one culture, and the evidence of their historical relationships with varied cultures and societies, demonstrates their potential to be associated with each of the world's contemporary cultures. Again, this is not to suggest that they will or should deny their own past cultural relationships; rather, it is to submit that the religious thought of the immediate future must confront the demands and implications of the presently and continually emerging world culture with its multi-cultured origins and its vari-cultured complexion.

A third path, which it appears the religions are required to follow in the immediate future, is one they have followed in the past, and are now following, without full realization of the direction in which it leads. This is the recognition by each religion that the universal nature of its essential themes forces a confrontation with rival claims to universal relevance. There is nothing completely new in the confrontation itself, nor is there much that is new in the suggestion that each religion must recognize that the rival claims are the result of real differences and not merely different ways of stating the same thing. However, we believe that the present world situation is new in the degree to which it makes this demand upon the religions and, also, in the way in which it makes such a confrontation available, yes, imperative, upon them. In the past, the religions of the West have been able in large measure to set the pace and conditions of the confrontation to suit their own desires. The religions of the East were, until a few centuries ago, generally removed from this confrontation except for the local struggles inevitable to any system of belief which claims to possess value. In any case, these religions today are not able to isolate themselves from the facts of world history, where before they were subjected to provincial or regional rivals in a condition equally urgent but less complex than today.

We have said that, in the immediate past, there has not been full awareness of the direction in which this path leads. Certainly there has not been a clear understanding of the contemporary cultural and religious situation throughout the world. Despite past experience in cultural relationships, the religions have, with rare exception, proceeded along this path in the tacit assumption that the goal is a complete destruction of their rivals or the essentials of the rival religion's understanding of itself. Again with rare exception, it has been assumed that the eventual attainment of supremacy by any of the religions would result not only in the great majority of mankind adopting its themes but also in the adjustment of the other cultures to its primary culture. During the greater part of the modern missionary period of Christian history, Christianity has generally been insistent upon this cultural adjustment, in some cases demonstrating little awareness of a distinction between its theological themes and western culture. Hinduism, while not as fully embarked upon a missionary program as Christianity, has not been able to distinguish the Hindu view of life, as generally lived in India, from the Hindu view of life presented in the Hindu themes we noted. Buddhism, just now in the earliest modern stages of following this path, has rarely evidenced the ability to articulate its message in a fashion relatively free from the eastern cultural context. Islam, despite its proven ability to draw diverse cultures into itself, has often covertly, if not overtly, furthered a cultural identification contrary to the cultural conditions of the modern world. In the case of each religion there are exceptions to the foregoing, and an argument can be made that it is the exceptions which furnish to each of these religions the key to the appropriate action they should take in this matter in the future.

The religious thought of the future, it would appear to us, must continue to follow this inescapable path of confrontation between the religions with the awareness that the emerging world or universal culture, by the very nature of its construction, will demand universal themes of any religious thought that seeks to be relevant in that culture. The religions we have considered maintain that their essential themes are universally applicable to all mankind in any cultural environment. If these themes are to play the role in the creation of this culture which each religion desires, then it follows that religious thought is required to express the themes within the new context of the emerging culture. To do this it will be necessary for the themes to be lifted above their still existent, provincial, cultural attachments as far as their inherent and essential nature permits. In the past decades the religions have become more aware of the independence of their themes from the strictures of their primary cultures, but they have not been able to implement this awareness in concrete terms and actions.

It will be the nature of a universal culture to demand universal religious themes because it will itself be constructed to serve all men in the local expressions of the total universal culture. The culture cannot attain the status of a world culture if it is not viable to all men, and the religious thought which is a part of that culture will have the same demand placed upon it. Since we would hold it obvious that any conceivable world culture of the next period of history will be a culture not devoid of religious themes, it follows that the themes themselves must also participate in the universality which will be a primary feature of the culture. If this is understood by the theologians and philosophers of the world religions, they will then be cognizant of the requirements placed upon them to establish the contemporary and future relevance of the religions they espouse and they will be prepared to meet the opportunity such a situation affords to the religions.

As a universal culture demands universal religious thought, so too religious thought that is universal in its content and relevance requires a universal culture to aid in the implementation of the truth present in the religious thought. It is difficult to conceive of either without the other as a primary supplement. The themes which constitute the intellectual and spiritual affirmations of a religion cannot be isolated from the human life, society, and process which is the culture of mankind. If they are thus removed from daily belief and action, they cease to exist as significant elements of the culture and something else arises to take their place.

The foregoing means that each of the religions we have considered is now required to apply the energies of its thought to the implementation of those aspects of the present historic cultures which are most important in the creation of a future universal culture and which will be amenable and helpful to the establishment of the essential themes of the religion. The religions must be selective among the various elements of their primary cultures, seeking to bring forth the cultural features which offer the best application of the themes of the religion to the life of mankind. As they search for those instances, they will undoubtedly discover that, in more than one case, the most significant example will be found in the expression of the essential theme in the environment of a secondary culture. Recognizing that the truth present within their themes is not absolutely tied to any one or group of temporal cultural manifestations, it will be incumbent upon them to associate and work with these as examples only of the value of religious thought for human life, not as absolutes which are not subject to alteration and possible supplementation in the future.

All of this is related to the confrontation between the religions, suggested as the essential characteristic of this third path of present and future religious thought. The religions will be confronting each other as they seek to put before the minds of men the pertinency of their separate messages, recognizing their differences, and, per-

haps, at the same time discovering similarities not yet fully comprehended. They will not, however, be enmeshed in argument or
discussion that remains at the level of theory without entering into
the sphere of human life at its cultural and social foundations. The
universal relevance of a religion, or of one or some of its essential
themes, will be established not by intellectual debate but by the
demonstration of such relevance through concrete instances of the
enrichment of individual and collective human life.

The proclamations to those outside the religion that only through
the particular faith will man's present and future correct relationship to the Divine be assured, have not in contemporary times
generally brought about the results each religion has sought. The
present cultural situation and the psychological and material condition of man, while not ruling out the strength of this religious
approach to man completely, demand that the religions establish
their relevance in a manner commensurate with the present beliefs
and conditions of mankind. This does not mean, as seems to be
generally assumed, that Christianity, for example, is required to
abandon its traditional and recurring themes. It does demand that
Christianity not place method above the truth and values of its
themes.

None of the religions, in their present advanced intellectual
thought, is primarily concerned with the method by which conversion to its beliefs is obtained as long as the method is not contrary
to the spirit of the truth it claims to possess. They are each concerned that men and women become aware of the truth. Confronting each other and the new emerging culture, they cannot demonstrate the relevance they claim without seriously considering the
nature of the contemporary situation to which they claim to be
relevant. Because of their localized origins and the nature of their
previous histories, they are not inevitably limited to pre- or non-
scientific man or society; they are not seeking to win the peoples of
one culture only; they are not limited in their own resources to a
primary or single culture; they are not fully expressed within
specific cultural manifestations to the exclusion of other manifestations; nor are they by their nature confined to the methods of their
past in the winning of adherents or the expression of their thought.
If they are irrevocably limited to any of the foregoing conditions

they are not universally relevant now nor possessed of a discernible potentiality to be so in the future.

As a universal culture will be a unity of varied contributions from many cultures, so too will universal theological and philosophical themes relevant to that culture be the result of a diversity within a harmony produced by the religions prepared to lose characteristics of their past in order to become the present and future vehicles of the themes of truth which brought them into existence. Following the path of confrontation with other claims contrary to and yet concomitant to their own, will, if done with sensitive awareness, aid them in discerning their own essential nature while throwing off the non-essentials which restrain them from their proper role as guiding themes and resources in the emerging culture of mankind. By their acknowledgment of the presence of revelation in all of human history—the first path we have suggested—and their awareness of the important role of culture as a means of the expression and demonstration of religious belief (the second path), the religions will be prepared to confront each other and the emerging culture with a breadth of understanding that, as that vital essence of revelation impinges upon the men and women of the future, will enable them to be sensitive to the inner content of the themes they articulate.

2

The paths of thought and procedure which lie before the world religions in the immediate and far future, no matter how essential they may be individually and collectively, are but the means to an end and not ends in themselves. Each possesses value in itself as an aid to the furtherance of the purpose of the religion which pursues it; none we have mentioned, or which may appear important to others now or in the future, must be confused with the ends which the religions seek.

It is at this point that each of the religions must be extremely careful not to fall into the error, all too often made in the past, as to the means whereby men and women are brought to a commitment to religious truth. The means are important because they are employed for purposes which are of ultimate significance to mankind. Each of the religions must seek to achieve its ends expressing its themes of thought and life with all appropriate means, but those means are of necessity the product of the ends they are designed to serve. The essence of religious thought and life does not arise from the manner in which it is expressed, rather the expression, if it is worthy of its originating impetus, is the resultant of the truth present in religious thought and life.

It is because the foregoing is absolutely fundamental to religion that the religious thought of the future must seek to relate itself to the whole of human life and not to only one aspect of it. We would agree with the many religious thinkers who point out that religion isolated from any activity or thought of human life is not religion as fundamentally conceived by religious men and women. This is not at all a comment that is new or limited to our time. The religious genius, saint, contemplative, activist, and average devout adherent—each has discovered for himself or herself the totality of religion and its demands upon the individual. And, as members of society, these religious individuals have each sought in their own way to bring religious truth into all of their relationships.

Religious thought in itself is not to be considered as *the* religious life. Nor should it be conceived as the only or primary means for the establishment of the revelancy of religion in the lives of men and women today or in the future. We have placed our emphasis upon it throughout our discussion because we believe it to be significant and important because of what it can do in the total task which confronts religion today. We do not hold it to be in itself the means which will bring to pass the end religion seeks. Given the nature of the present condition of mankind and the highly probable ethos in which men and women shall live in the foreseeable future, the intellectual expressions of religion will play an increasingly important role in the demonstration of religious relevance. Be that expression primarily theological, philosophical, aesthetic, scientific, or social, the degree to which it attains intellectual clarity and pertinence will determine in large measure the extent of its contribution to the religious life of mankind.

However the religious history of the past and present demonstrates that, behind the intellectual speculation and expressions of religion, there is something which is primary in its impetus to the whole of the religious life. Sensitive and empathetic consideration of each of the religions reveals to the perceptive observer the presence of a human awareness of a divine activity from which spring the many facets of human religiosity. Throughout recorded time men have lived with a consciousness of a divine concern for man and his history. They have not believed that they live alone as individuals, and they have not thought that the society and culture of which they were a part were removed from this concern. Three of the religions we have considered, and the Mahayana expression of Buddhism, have at the base of all of their themes the conviction that the Divine has been made manifest in human life, and that human life is absolutely and totally different than it would have been without this divine activity. Even Theravada Buddhism, though it may object to our terminology, and perhaps to what we are seeking to express, finds its origin and much of its appeal in the figure of one who, as a result of his full perception of truth, was moved to an infinite compassion for all living creatures. The Lord Buddha, by his enlightenment, made known to his fellow men that truth is not isolated from man but is available to suffering mankind and its predicament.

The theological and philosophical expressions of the essence of a religion may easily become engaged in systematization and verbalization to the lesser awareness of the richness of the aesthetic, emotional, personal ingredients of religion. What we would consider good theology and religious philosophy, that religious thought which has moved men's minds and strengthened their religious sensitivities, has not lost this awareness. The religious thought of the future will be successful in the meeting of its duty only if it keeps alive and fresh the awareness of the emotional depth and grandeur which is present in all vital religious experience.

Among all of the present potential ingredients of the emerging world culture, the major religions appear to us as the primary potential sources for the institution and development of the consciousness of the divine activity and the compassion for human life which flows from that activity. Unless the religions act, by clear and pertinent expression of their themes and by other activities, in inculcating that awareness into the individuals who shall compose that culture, it will at best be a feeble and limited force in world society.

What we have termed the divine activity and compassion for life is to be found in the central figures that are related to and inherent in the theological-philosophical themes of each of the religions we have considered. Despite all else that can and must be said to adequately describe the central beliefs of each religion, the underlying impetus behind each religion's primary spiritual and intellectual experience is an awareness of a compassion for human life underlying all existence. The truth is understood to have entered into man's historical experience. In the case of each religion this is conceived differently, either in theory and/or in the nature of the event wherein the truth was most clearly revealed to men. Nevertheless, believing ourselves to be conscious of the width of the difference between the various religions and their themes, we would hold that each of them would maintain that a primary essence of their origin and of their historical message to mankind lies in the compassion for human life which is inherent to the truth, underlying all existence. The God of grace who seeks men and women through the medium of historical events and personal encounter, Allah the Compassionate and Merciful, the Nirmāṇakāya who comes into human life and its suffering as the manifestation of the Dharmakāya, the Avataras who bring to men and women the grace of the Bhagavat, the Bodhisattvas who deny to themselves the full experience of Nirvana until all creatures have been brought to its peace, the human beings chosen by the Divine as the instruments for the bringing of revelation to mankind, the men and women who through their own experience of the divine revelation or their own encounter with truth are led by compassion to convey it to others— these are the central figures, personalities, the elements which furnish the impetus to religion and the experience on which it is based. Individually or collectively, they serve to bring men and women into a consciousness of the religious understanding of life and its meaning, an understanding designed, among other things, to instill within human life and culture a compassion for all mankind and a sensitivity to the rich potentiality of individuals and their collective cultural creations.

From this religious apprehension, perceived by men and women in their individual religious experiences and strengthened by their collective intellectual and cultic expressions, there comes the radiancy of commitment which makes religion relevant to them and, through them, to the culture of which they are a part. The experience of individual encounter with the Divine, with truth, is the foundation for all subsequent religious expression. The religions we would consider most pertinent to the contemporary world and its problems find, in the intellectual statements of their themes of belief, the inevitable results of the prior experience and not the experience itself. Collective religious belief and religious activity may lead the individual to his own religious experience. The experience itself, however, would appear to require ultimately a personal event if it is to possess the depth and purpose which man has come to associate with religion at its highest level. And from the religiously committed individual, with his absolute conviction of the relevance of his own experience for all men, there comes an inevitable challenge to others to enter into the experience for themselves.

The religious thought of the future, as that of the past, has to have the consciousness of this personal religious experience at the very center of its own formulations and understanding of its task. Without this awareness it is all too obvious that the religious thought of any age will be sterile and without relevance to mankind. Individual men and the cultures which they produce are dependent upon religious thought which arises out of religious experience. They are cheated of that thought and its potential richness for them if it is created without the support of religious experience which, while not anti-intellectual, is far greater in scope and content than can be confined to the rational alone.

3

In a penetrating discussion of "Why Religions Die," the late Professor James Bissett Pratt has suggested that those religions of history which have disappeared from human society were systems of belief and action which lost their relevance to the ever-changing conditions of human life.[1] The religions of Egypt, of Babylonia, and the classical Graeco-Roman world were each religions which did not possess the necessary sensitivity to be sufficiently aware of the changing needs of men's minds and spiritual requirements. Nor did they possess thematic resources which enabled them to convey to their changing cultures the elements which had once made them religions of significance to their adherents. And, most revealing of all, in the circumstances of their own downfall, each demonstrated an iron bound conservatism which prevented it from continuing in partnership with the accompanying culture which was being forced to adjust to new conditions. Referring to the age old religion of Egypt, Pratt maintains, "In the last form of the religion none of the ancient usages and ideas had been discarded, regardless of their inconsistency with newer elements." [2] And he contends that "the real cause of its death was its age-long irrational conservatism." [3] So, too, "Babylonian religion perished because it was unable to satisfy the intellectual and ideal needs of its followers as well as Zoroastrianism and Greek philosophy did." [4] "Paganism died at last because it had been weakened by the thousand-year attack of Naturalism, because the world's spiritual needs had been gradually and greatly modified and enlarged since the early days of Greece and Rome, and because the old religion was not able to throw off the hampering bands of irrational tradition and could not satisfy the new longings of the day as completely as they were satisfied by the rival that came up from Palestine." [5]

As against these religions, Pratt considers the case of the religion associated with the Vedas of India. Here he sees one primary difference between Hindu religious thought and other developed religions which have disappeared from men's minds. The Vedic religion and its hymns and concepts were believed to be inspired, but they were not bound in an ironclad manner which prevented the discovery in them of new meaning, a meaning commensurate with the developing religious experience and insights of men. "Thus the religion of the Veda did not die; that which in it was vital and true cast off its old shell and clothed itself in more suitable expression, with no break in the continuity of its life . . ." [6] He concludes his essay with the assertion that Christianity must choose the Vedic way, "the way of constant spiritual reinterpretation," which leads "to life which is self-perpetuating, self-renewing, and which, for the individual and for the world, may be eternal." [7]

Our discussion of Christianity, Hinduism, Buddhism, and Islam has sought to remind us of the present circumstances of each of the religions as it confronts a world which is not the same as the one in which it began nor in which it has developed to its present state nor in which it will exist in the probable future. The primary revelation, or revelations, and the religious experience which gave birth to the religion, are together the central and continuing impetus which gives the religion its *raison d'etre*. Yet in each case that revelation and the experience resulting from it has been enriched by a never-ending religious experience among the men and women who have found the religion to be relevant to their lives.

These religions owe much of their contemporary existence to their thinkers who throughout the centuries have in each new circumstance recognized the need and possessed the foresight to reinvigorate the themes of the religion in the light of man's need of the truth present in the religion's message. Ever aware of the values of the past, but not limited by the forms in which those values have been expressed, these seminal theologians and philosophers have confronted the mandate their time placed upon dynamic religion with the confidence that their religion was the resultant of a truth not bound by time or place and adequate to meet any adversary. As every man is the product of his time, so these thinkers were limited in the expression of that which they conceived to be timeless. Some may have believed their formulation of the essential themes of their faith to have been as timeless as the theme itself; we have all too often made the same erroneous assumption. The day in which we live will not allow us to continue in that error, nor will it permit us the luxury of believing that any of these religions will be relevant to future generations without our own attempt to make them so in ours.

The future of religious thought is hazardous at best. The history of religion demonstrates that it is often just when such hazard exists that the best religious thought, the insight into recurring themes and significant expression of them, becomes most relevant to men. The religious experience which underlies human life is an experience that is enriched in the midst of doubt and trouble. But it cannot possess the relevance which is inherent to it, the significance to human life and culture which it inevitably and properly seeks, without taking unto itself the forms of expression which are meaningful in the ethos of each new generation of mankind.

The mandate of the present age upon religion is not a mandate which arises alone from the nature of the present and the probability of the future. Rather, in conjunction with these, it rises ultimately from the mandate that each religion is reminded of by its recurring themes and its experience with them. It comes from themes which have their origin in the past, continue to rise afresh in the present, and demand to be made newly relevant in the future. The essentials of the religious thought of the future will result from a sensitive tension within the religious thinkers of today and tomorrow, a tension between their own religious experience, the themes of their religious tradition, and the conditions of the culture which surrounds them. The future of religious thought in the culture and conditions which are emerging, is dependent now upon the renewed application of the human intellect to the truth which is revealed in the religions of the world today.

NOTES

[1] *University of California Publications in Philosophy*, 16, No. 5, 95-124.
[2] *Ibid.*, p. 100. By permission.
[3] *Ibid.*, p. 101. By permission.
[4] *Ibid.*, p. 103. By permission.
[5] *Ibid.*, pp. 109 f. By permission.
[6] *Ibid.*, p. 121. By permission.
[7] *Ibid.*, p. 124. By permission.

INDEX

* Also available in limited clothbound edition.

The American Assembly Series

Classics in History Series

* Also available in limited clothbound edition.

* Also available in limited clothbound edition.

* Also available in limited clothbound edition.